GOLD RUSH WOMEN

CLAIRE RUDOLF MURPHY & JANE G. HAIGH

Hillside Press

For Jane Williams and all pioneer women of Alaska, and for my daughters, Anna Berry and Molly Haigh. —J.H.

To the Fairbanks Fifteen and Chilkoot '95: Carol, Katie, Laura, and Ron Johnson; Claire, Conor, Megan, and Bob Murphy; Gin, Jamo, and Jane Parrish; Katie, Jim, Lisa, and Theresa Villano.—C.R.M.

Originally published by Alaska Northwest Books®, Portland, Oregon, 1997.

Second edition published by Hillside Press, 2012.
Third printing, 2018

Library of Congress Control Number: 2012935946

ISBN: 978-0-9627530-5-3

Design: Elizabeth Watson
Maps: Gray Mouse Graphics
Production: Susan Dupèrè

Photographs: The photos in this book are from numerous institutional and private collections. Photo credits are listed on page 123.
Front cover: Center: Ethel Berry, c. 1897; Left, top to bottom: Klondike Kate, c. 1900; Anna De Graf, c. 1898; Sinrock Mary, c. 1910; Kate Carmack, c. 1898. Page 1: Ethel Berry, c. 1897. 3: Alma Nelson. 119: Alice McDonald's children, Sigrid and Donald, Iditarod, c. 1912. 122: Harriet Pullen, Skagway, c. 1920. 123: Woman in Dawson City, c. 1905. 124: Skagway interior, 1900.

Hillside Press
1573 Union St.
Manchester, NY 03104
www.janehaigh.com

Printed in China

A change had come over Mother. I could sense it even then, at the age of five. I had worried about her, tried to take care of her on the long trip to Alaska, but now all at once I could see she was able to take care of herself. She looked as fragile and delicate as Swedish blown glass, but she was made of harder stuff. She had the courage of all the pioneer women who followed their men to the frontier North. Some of them faltered and turned back; others, like my mother, stayed on and adapted themselves to the rugged life and came in time to love it. They turned a wilderness of brawling gold camps into a decent land of schools and churches and homes. My mother was as strong in her own way as my dad. In some ways, as it turned out, she was even stronger.

—Klondy Nelson, from Daughter of the Gold Rush

CONTENTS

1

2

▲ *After Anna De Graf's
journey over the Chilkoot
Trail in 1897, her clothes
were in tatters, her feet
wrapped in rags.*

▶ *A Miss Lindstrom from
Fairbanks clowns around with
miners while on a hunting trip in
the Kantishna District, 1914.*

◀ *Polly Anderson, the owner of a fox farm on Wonder Lake near Kantishna in the 1920s.*

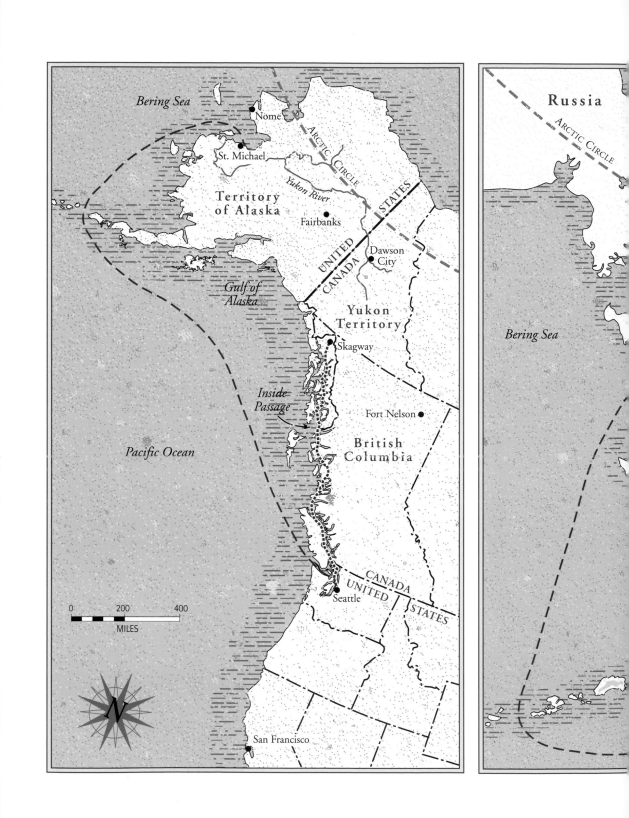

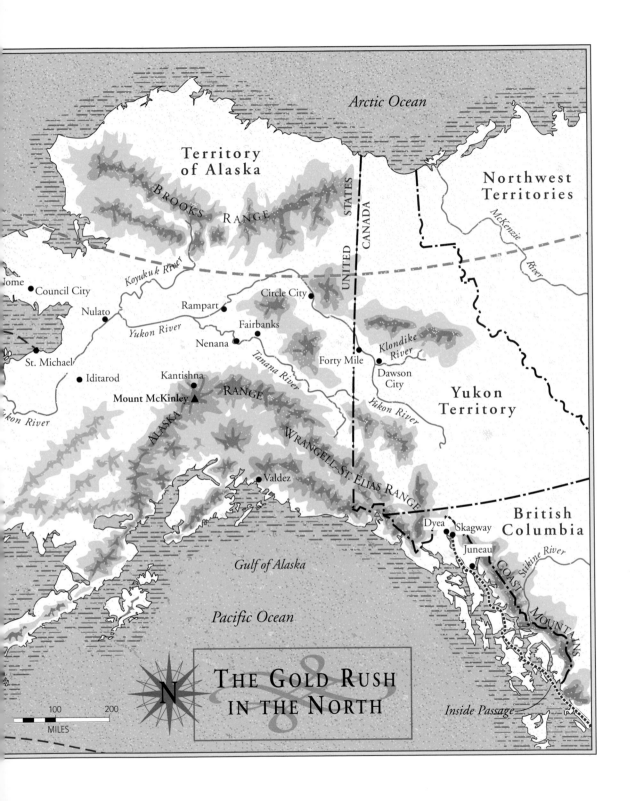

THE GOLD RUSH IN THE NORTH

INTRODUCTION

WOMEN IN THE NORTH

Popular myth portrays the gold rush North as a place where men battled nature in a struggle for gold. While most histories concentrate on the gold rush experience from the male prospectors' perspective, in fact thousands of women were also drawn to Alaska and the Yukon seeking not only gold but the many and varied opportunities this new land offered.

A nationwide economic depression in the United States in 1893 spurred the northern migration. When word of the fantastic gold discoveries in Canada's Yukon Territory reached the outside world in 1897, women eagerly set off for the Klondike as equal partners with their husbands, in the company of strange men, or even unescorted. Of the hordes of people who stampeded North, one in ten was female.

Fifty years earlier women had traveled West in covered wagons, most often accompanied by their husband and children or friends. They too overcame great adversity to start new lives. But the pioneer movement on the Plains was more often a family affair, with the promise of free land and a new home at the end of the trail. In the North, disease and Indian attacks weren't the greatest challenges facing stampeders: the experience of women in that wilderness was shaped by the brutal cold, rugged territory, and vast unpeopled distances.

◄◄◄ Two women with their bakery and cafe under construction in Discovery City, near Otter Creek in the Iditarod District, c. 1911.

◄◄ Young career women pose for a group portrait in Dawson City after the gold rush boomtown had become a settled community, c. 1905.

▲ Mine and hotel owner Jenny Cleveland in dogsled, with a friend at Dome City, on the gold creeks outside of Fairbanks, c. 1910.

Living and traveling in the Northland was filled with extreme hardships. Women who journeyed to the Klondike, for example, traversed the Chilkoot or White Pass Trails on foot or on horseback, carrying heavy packs. Like their male counterparts, women navigated steep rocky trails and rafted swift-moving streams, enduring cold, wet conditions, meager rations, and numbing fatigue. And like male stampeders, women hoped for instant riches.

With few exceptions, the women who arrived in the North did not find the streets paved with gold. But those willing to work hard did find opportunities to make money. They discovered that the domestic skills of cooking, sewing, laundering, and housekeeping were in great demand—and people were willing to pay well for the services. Women like Belinda Mulrooney seized the chance to open boarding houses, restaurants, or hotels. Professional women came North, working as newspaper reporters, teachers, nurses, and entertainers. Many women came as wives of prospectors; a few brought their children with them and even fewer, like Lucille Hunter, risked giving birth along the trail.

▶ *Harriet Pullen was a tireless promoter of her fabulous Pullen House in Skagway, the most elegant hotel in Alaska, c. 1920. Today in downtown Skagway all that can be seen of the Pullen House are the remains of a fireplace. But the glory of the hotel and its hostess live on in each retelling of the town's golden past.*

12

INTRODUCTION

Women staked or leased claims, working solo mines or hiring men to do the work, like Martha Louise Black, who faced great opposition from male miners. There were experienced women miners, too, like Nellie Cashman, who had lived in boomtowns all over the West.

Twenty years before the Klondike strike, Koyukon Athabascan women like Margaret Mayo left their families to marry the first traders exploring the vast Alaskan Interior. These Native women demonstrated that survival in the North Country greatly depended on knowledge of the land and hunting, fishing, trapping, and gathering skills. They taught their non-Native husbands how to work with nature to harvest the bounty it provided. The first white women to arrive in the Interior also learned crucial skills from these Native women.

Whatever their backgrounds, the Northland's pioneer women helped to form a new social order. The women's stories featured in this book cover the history of the gold rushes in Alaska and the Yukon Territory, between the 1880s and the early 1900s. In Chapter 1 we introduce women who were ahead of their time, the

▲ *Two women stroll by cabins on the outskirts of Dome City, near Fairbanks, c. 1910. While the cabins were primitive, power poles indicate that they did have electricity.*

Athabascan women who married early traders and the few white women who arrived in the Yukon Basin before the Klondike gold rush. These women together helped to form Northern communities of Forty Mile and Circle City in the 1880s and early 1890s. Chapter 2 features women who helped discover the Klondike gold in 1896 and who were able to capitalize on its riches. It also presents women who survived treacherous trips North in '97–98 to reach Dawson, cutting ties to home in the process. Chapter 3 describes how particular women seized the unique opportunities of the frontier, making as much money as men. Chapter 4 profiles women in the Alaska gold rush communities of Rampart and Nome at the end of the century. And Chapter 5 tells how when gold was found near the present-day site of Fairbanks, many left Nome and Dawson to settle in the Interior, and Fairbanks became an enduring family community.

These women's gold rush experiences affected the rest of their lives. Women like Emilie Tremblay found riches and remained in the North when the gold rush ended, continuing to mine but also starting schools or businesses and raising children. Others like Belinda Mulrooney and Frances Fitz took their fortunes with them and left, but never forgot their Northern adventures. Another group of women, like Bridget Mannion, stayed only a brief period

	1849	1861	1871	1873	1880	1886	1888
GOLD RUSH TIME LINE	■ Russian mining engineer discovers gold and coal on Kenai Peninsula.	■ Gold discovered near Wrangell. ■ First lode claim in Alaska filed at Kasaan near Ketchikan.	■ Gold discovered near Sitka.	■ American traders arrive on Yukon River.	■ The Tlingit agree to allow prospectors to use Chilkoot Pass. ■ Major gold strike leads to founding of Juneau.	■ Gold discovered on Fortymile River in Interior Alaska.	■ Gold strikes on Kenai Peninsula.

of time, but long enough to put their old lives behind them and make a fresh start. On the other hand, tragedy struck some women: the riches from gold brought great sadness to Kate Carmack's life.

Gold rush women were of all ages. They were married, single, and divorced. They came from all parts of the world and all levels of society. In compiling this book, we started with women who had written their own memoirs, but little history was available for most of the women featured here. Many of our profiles were developed by piecing together small bits of information found in a variety of sources—census records, newpaper articles, government documents, gold rush histories, and family stories recounted by their descendants. Sometimes even birth and death dates were impossible to find.

The profiles included here were selected to reveal the depth and variety of women's roles in the North during this consequential era. Women who participated in the gold rush discovered that they possessed more skills and strength than they had ever imagined. With a new sense of confidence and growing self-reliance, they not only survived but also flourished. Their stories offer a context within which to understand the lives of hundreds of other gold rush women. Because these women followed their dreams, not just of gold but of a life of greater independence and opportunity, their stories can inspire us today.

1893	1896	1897	1898	1899	1902	1914
▪ Gold discovered near Hope and Circle City.	▪ George and Kate Carmack, Tagish Charlie, and Skookum Jim make discovery on Bonanza Creek, setting off Klondike gold rush.	▪ SS *Excelsior* and SS *Portland* arrive at San Francisco and Seattle loaded with Klondike gold—the stampede begins.	▪ Stampeders stream over Chilkoot Pass and White Pass, heading for the Klondike. ▪ Soapy Smith shot and killed in Skagway. ▪ Major gold strike on Seward Peninsula near Nome. ▪ Prospectors arrive at Valdez en route to the Klondike gold fields via the All-American Route.	▪ White Pass & Yukon Route Railroad, begun in 1898, reaches White Pass Summit. ▪ Mining begins on the beaches of Nome.	▪ Gold strike leads to the founding of Fairbanks.	▪ Gold discovered at Livengood— the last rush.

Chapter 1

GOLD IN THE YUKON BASIN
WILDERNESS COMMUNITIES

When the United States purchased Alaska from Russia in 1867, the territory was largely unknown and unexplored. Americans Arthur Harper, Alfred Mayo, and Leroy Napoleon "Jack" McQuesten had heard about the potential of the Yukon River Basin: it was a rich untouched region for fur trapping and there were whispered rumors of gold. After a two-year overland journey, the three men arrived in Fort Yukon, Alaska, in 1873 to explore the river basin. By the following summer, two of the three men had married Athabascan women from Interior Alaska's Nulato–Tanana area and all had joined forces to establish several trading posts for the Alaska Commercial Company along the Yukon River.

These trading posts became all-important hubs of activity for those who lived in this remote region—Natives, missionaries, trappers, and miners. Prospectors were able to get the supplies and equipment necessary for gold mining. The traders even financed some prospectors' efforts by extending a winter's goods to them on credit, a practice known as "grubstaking." Then if a miner struck gold, the trader would receive a share of the profits. It was largely through the presence and generosity of entrepreneurs such as Harper, Mayo, and McQuesten that over the next twenty years, gold was discovered in the Yukon Basin.

◄◄◄ *Forty Mile in 1894 had two trading posts, a mission, a Royal Canadian Mounted Police station, businesses, and houses—all built of logs.*

◄◄ *McQuesten's store at Circle City, Alaska, c. 1898, was an important trading post of the gold rush. Jack McQuesten, sometimes known as the Father of the Yukon, stands at far left, behind the dog.*

▲ *This family in the Yukon enjoys a fine meal in their tent.*

The Native wives of the traders and prospectors helped to develop a new Northern way of life that combined traditional Native foods, clothing, and beliefs with the technology, religion, and habits of the Euro-Americans—creating an ingenious, synthesized lifestyle that allowed isolated pioneers to thrive. While these Native women lived with their families in log cabins, learned to cook on cast-iron woodstoves, planted vegetable gardens, traveled by steamboat, and had their children baptized, they also used Native animal skin-sewing techniques to make their family's clothing, and often supplemented their income by sewing mukluks, parkas, pants, mittens, and hats for sale or trade to other prospectors. To the sparse miner's diet of beans, bacon, and biscuits, they added the fish they caught, the caribou they hunted, the rabbits they snared, and the berries and edible/medicinal plants they gathered.

The town of Forty Mile in Alaska became the first major frontier settlement on the Yukon River after two prospectors found substantial quantities of gold there in 1886. The women who lived at Forty Mile included the Athabascan wives of prospectors and traders and the first white women to travel up the Yukon River or over the Chilkoot Pass. The community became close-knit: everyone traded at the post, attended social events together, and sent their children to school at the local Anglican mission. These women had established more than community—they had created civilization in the wilderness.

But existence along the rugged Yukon was harsh. In the winter of 1894–95, the women living there faced extreme conditions and isolation, never staying in one place long, often moving when gold was discovered elsewhere. While the precious metal was being taken from the hills and creeks surrounding Forty Mile, trader Jack McQuesten encouraged further prospecting. In 1893, Pitka Pavalof and Sergei Cherosky found gold on Birch Creek, and in two years the new Alaskan settlement of Circle City on the creek grew into the biggest log cabin city in the world, with over a thousand residents. Then in August 1896, a major gold strike was discovered in the Klondike River region and Circle City and Forty Mile became virtually deserted.

"Circle City is dead—dead as a doorpost. The Birch Creek Mines are as good as ever, but they are simply nothing compared with the Klondike."
—School teacher, Anna Fulcomer, 1897

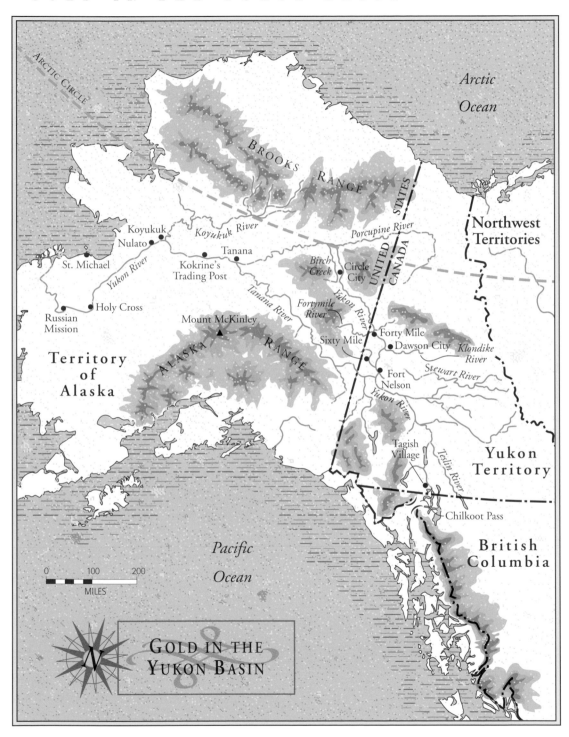

ARCTIC CIRCLE

Arctic Ocean

BROOKS RANGE

Northwest Territories

Koyukuk
Nulato
Koyukuk River
Tanana
Porcupine River
St. Michael
Kokrine's Trading Post
Birch Creek
Circle City
UNITED STATES
CANADA
Yukon River
Holy Cross
Tanana River
Fortymile River
Yukon River
Russian Mission
Mount McKinley
Sixty Mile
Forty Mile
Dawson City
Klondike River

Territory of Alaska
ALASKA RANGE
Fort Nelson
Stewart River
Yukon River

Yukon Territory

Tagish Village
Teslin River

Pacific Ocean

Chilkoot Pass

British Columbia

0   100   200
MILES

N

GOLD IN THE YUKON BASIN

KATHERINE JAMES McQUESTEN 1860–1918

Bridging Two Cultures

▲ *Kate McQuesten and her children Henry, Elizabeth, Julia, and Crystal in 1898, shortly before their move to Berkeley, California. There the children were tutored in English and manners, and graduated from Berkeley High School.*

In 1874 Satejdenalno, a young Russian-Athabascan woman, was living at Kokrine's, a trading post between the villages of Tanana and Nulato at one of the most beautiful spots along the Yukon River. Life in the small Interior Alaska settlement revolved around "old man Kokrine," one of the few Russian traders remaining on the river after the 1867 purchase of Alaska by the United States. As a girl, Satejdenalno had attended school at the Russian Mission at Ikogmiut. Katherine, or Kate, as she came to be called, could speak Russian as well as her Koyukon Athabaskan language.

That summer fourteen-year-old Kate met Jack McQuesten, a tall, barrel-chested man with a flowing mustache. An American, McQuesten had left New Hampshire to search for gold in Canada's Fraser River Valley. Over a four-year period, McQuesten traveled 2,000 miles overland to reach the Yukon River. He and his two partners, Al Mayo and Arthur Harper, planned to establish trading posts along the Yukon River for the Alaska Commercial Company. On their way to St. Michael, they stopped at Kokrine's.

Al Mayo married a woman named Margaret that summer, and Margaret's cousin Jennie married Arthur Harper. The two couples opened a new trading post at Old Station near Tanana. McQuesten traveled a thousand miles up the Yukon to establish Fort Reliance, just six miles from the present site of Dawson. Four years later,

KATHERINE McQUESTEN

1860–1918

Kate married the 42-year-old McQuesten. Over the years, Kate and Jack moved from post to post, following trading opportunities and developments in the mining communities. In the summer of 1886, the McQuestens, Mayos, and Harpers established Fort Nelson at the mouth of the Stewart River in the Yukon Territory. Later at Forty Mile, a gold rush camp near the Alaskan border that grew into a large and active community, Kate was known for her bountiful vegetable gardens. She even tried harnessing a moose to her plow to turn the soil. As the wife of Forty Mile's most important trader, Kate was an intermediary between the Native and white communities. She organized many social events, some of which were attended by the few white women in the region, including Bridget Mannion and Anna De Graf.

In 1894, following discoveries of gold on Birch Creek, Kate and Jack established the Alaska Commercial Company store at Circle City. There Kate gave birth to the eighth of her eleven children in a tent outside her house, according to Athabascan custom. All of the older children were sent Outside (outside Alaska) to attend school.

In the spring of 1897, news of the Klondike gold strike emptied the town of Circle City. Jack, fearing the dismal conditions and possible food shortages like those in the new boom town of Dawson, moved his family to California. Kate, having already adapted to many different settlements on the Yukon River, once again embraced a new life, this time in a large Victorian mansion far from her home region, in the bustling town of Berkeley.

Kate McQuesten's life reflected the enormous change the Northland experienced because of the discovery of gold: the North was altered from the remote, traditional home of her Athabascan people to a land inhabited by prospectors and white merchants. As Jack McQuesten's wife and partner, she was one of the first women in the Northern gold rushes to work toward establishing community among the Natives and the newcomers in her homeland. After Jack died in 1910, Kate's education and her experience in the trading business enabled her to manage her considerable estate. She lived in Berkeley with two of her daughters until her death in 1918.

JENNIE BOSCO HARPER ALEXANDER c. 1860–1921

A Return to Her Roots

▲ *Koyukon Athabascan Jennie Harper Alexander was married to trader Arthur Harper from 1874 until 1897. Committed to her cultural traditions, Jennie later returned to her Native community, remarried, and became a respected Athabascan elder in Tanana.*

Seentahna, whose Western name was Jennie Bosco, was living at Koyukuk Station during the summer of 1874. Her Koyukon River people, who had been suffering from famine, were encamped on the banks of the Yukon River to fish when fourteen-year-old Jennie met and married thirty-nine-year-old trader Arthur Harper.

Jennie and Arthur joined her cousin, Margaret Mayo, and Margaret's husband, Al Mayo, in establishing a post at Tanana, near the traditional trading site of Nuklukayet. Though married to a white trader, Jennie never abandoned her Native traditions, perhaps because she hadn't been educated at Russian Mission or experienced life at Kokrine's trading post. She continued to speak the Koyukon language and to rely on her skills gathering berries, snaring rabbits, and drying fish.

While Arthur Harper's trading activities supported their growing family, at heart he was still a prospector. He made frequent prospecting trips and was the first white man to explore many of the creeks and rivers of the Upper Yukon Basin. Arthur frequently left Jennie alone while he searched for gold, and his absences could last for two years.

Although Jennie objected, Arthur insisted their first seven children be sent Outside to be educated. Their last child, Walter, was born in 1893. Jennie and Arthur separated permanently in 1895, and Jennie moved back to Tanana with Walter, who was raised in the traditional way, learning to hunt and fish. Arthur Harper went on to Dawson and remarried; he died in Arizona in 1897.

At sixteen Walter attended St. Mark's Mission in Nenana, where his outdoor skills and pleasant personality attracted the attention of the explorer, Episcopal missionary, and (later) Archdeacon of Alaska, Hudson Stuck, who adopted him as his travel companion and camp assistant. In 1912, Walter accompanied Stuck on one of the explorer's greatest expeditions: Jennie's Athabascan son became the first person to set foot on the summit of Mount McKinley.

Jennie later married Nenana Native Robert Alexander. She is remembered as a respected elder and potlatch orator, speaking only Athabascan in that phase of her life. Few people knew the part she had played in the opening of the gold rush. The Native family values that she instilled in all of her children inspired them all to return to Alaska's Interior, where the Harper family continues to thrive today. Jennie died in Tanana in 1921.

GOLD IN JUNEAU

Gold rushers heading for the Interior often stopped in Juneau, where they saw and heard one of the richest gold mining operations in the world—the Treadwell Mines on nearby Douglas Island. The hard-rock gold tied up in the rock itself, called ore, was mined in a huge pit called the Glory Hole. To extract the gold, each of over 500 half-ton stamps pounded the ore ninety-eight times per minute, creating a constant roar that could be heard like thunder twenty-four hours a day. By 1892 two new mining companies were incorporated down the beach and each added new stamp mills of their own. By 1899 there were 880 stamps processing ore from four different mines.

In 1894, the year Anna De Graf and the Snow family arrived in Juneau, the mines employed almost 300 men and yielded nearly $1 million. Additional mining was being carried out in the mountains above Juneau. All of this activity supported a thriving town of Juneau. Yet some of the miners, hearing tales of free placer claims farther north, drifted up and over the passes to prospect the Yukon Basin.

ANNA DeGRAF

Sewing Machine Sourdough

▲ *Anna De Graf after hiking the Chilkoot Trail, 1897, with her clothes tattered, her feet wrapped in rags. When she landed in Circle City in October 1894, in a party including a baker and his wife from Juneau, she said "Our arrival swelled the number of white women in the settlement from six to eight."*

Fifty-five-year-old Anna De Graf climbed the rugged Chilkoot Pass in early spring of 1894, walking with the help of a crutch, her sore feet wrapped in rags. With her sewing machine and a feather bed from her native Saxony, she traveled over the rocky route toward the Yukon in search of her youngest son, George, who had gone to Alaska in 1892 in search of gold.

Anna had boarded a boat from Seattle to Juneau, to find her son when she hadn't heard from him in several months. She remained in Juneau for two years, working as a seamstress and waiting for news. In the spring of 1894, Anna heard that a young man named De Graf had passed through the Interior. She immediately joined a group heading out on the old Tlingit trail over the Chilkoot Pass and down the Yukon River to Circle City, site of the most recent gold strike.

Challenge was not new to Anna. She left Germany in 1867 and came to America at the age of twenty-three, having already survived a revolution and the death of her first child. On the East Coast, she and her husband lost everything in the panic of 1873 and so her husband went West to seek gold, but he was killed. Anna moved to Seattle, where she worked as a dressmaker to support her five children.

Hiking over the 3,700-foot Chilkoot Pass, she wore a heavy skirt and layered petticoats, a blouse, warm jacket, cap, and heavy shoes. She described her journey in

ANNA De GRAF

1839–1930

her autobiography, *Pioneering the Yukon*: "From Sheep Camp we entered a canyon and continued the climb upward to what was called the Scales. We had to climb over and around jagged rocks, sometimes jumping from one to another like mountain goats. From the Scales it was almost perpendicular to the summit. It was sunset when we reached the top and a wonderful panorama met our eyes. There were seven glaciers in view and the sun shining on the ice played all the colors of the rainbow. I was so impressed I felt I could never go on. Some of the party were impatient and wanted to push ahead. 'Oh, come on,' they said. 'We don't care about scenery, we want to find gold.' I exclaimed aloud, 'My God, how beautiful you have made the world!' We camped there overnight and the next morning started over the deep crevasses in the ice. One misstep might have sent us to oblivion."

During her 800-mile journey down the Yukon River, Anna inquired at the settlements of Sixty Mile and Forty Mile for word of her son. She finally arrived in Circle City during an October snowstorm. Her party's arrival increased the number of white women in town from six to eight. Several hundred miners had come in from the creeks to spend the winter in town, but Anna's son was not among them.

Waiting out the winter, Anna soon got work from trader Jack McQuesten sewing tents to sell at his Alaska Commercial Company store. She also made clothing for the miners and dance-hall girls. Involved with every aspect of the community, she helped teacher Anna Fulcomer start the town's first school.

In the spring of 1896, when the Alaska Commercial Company supply boat arrived in Circle City, Anna decided to abandon her search. She sold her sewing machine and left Alaska for San Francisco, taking her earnings in gold dust. When she turned in her dust to the mint, she received $1,200 for her two years of hard work. She had not struck it rich, but her savings were a considerable stake in that depression era.

Anna spent the winter in San Francisco with her daughter. But, still longing for word of her son, she said, "When the news of the

My mother used to say, "You must howl with the wolves when you are with the wolves," and so I made the best of things up there. Many times my heart did bump— I was so frightened— but I pretended I was just the bravest thing in the world, and I got through it all right. And now as an old woman, if I were young instead with no one to depend on me, I would certainly go back to that Yukon country and prospect and make myself independently rich.

—Anna De Graf

▲ Circle City was under construction in the summer of 1894. Two dozen Native women were among the original residents. In 1895, several hundred miners wintered over along with a few Native men.

strike on the Klondike fired my brain, I joined the stampede—not for the gold in the ground but because I wanted my son, and I knew that I must earn my way on my travels." So Anna bought another sewing machine, bolts of fabric and dressmaking supplies, and headed North once more in 1897.

Altogether, Anna spent more than twenty years on the Last Frontier, living in Juneau, Circle City, Dawson, Whitehorse, and Skagway. She left Alaska for good in 1917, never knowing the fate of her son. But after all her years of hard work, Anna couldn't sit still. She worked as a wardrobe manager for showman Alex Pantages in San Francisco, where she died at age ninety-one.

SOURDOUGH

Carried by many early-day pioneers, this versatile, yeasty starter was used to make bread, doughnuts and hot cakes. Sourdough cookery remains popular in Alaska today. Because the sourdough supply is replenished after each use, it can remain active and fresh indefinitely. A popular claim of sourdough cooks is that their batches trace back to pioneers at the turn of the century. The name also came to be applied to any Alaska or Yukon old-timer.

—The Alaska Almanac, 1996

*These two Athabascan women at Fort Yukon still live a traditional
subsistence life-style during gold rush days, though they wear Western-style dresses
and live in a canvas tent purchased from traders.*

In the traditional subsistence lifestyle of
Native Americans, all food, clothing, shelter,
tools, and fuel came from the natural
environment. Manufactured foods and goods
were unknown or rarely used. For at least
10,000 years, the Eskimo, Indian, and Aleut
peoples of Alaska and Northern Canada had
lived off the land in the harsh North as skilled
hunters and gatherers.

The Athabascan Indians of the Interior
were nomadic, following the food sources from
season to season. At summer fish camps along
major rivers, they caught and dried salmon and
other fish. In fall hunting camps, they hunted
caribou and moose, drying the meat for winter
food and tanning the skins for clothing. In the
winter, they trapped beaver and snared rabbits.

The Eskimo and Aleut peoples of Alaska's
coastal regions relied primarily on the rich
resources of the sea and the rivers. They hunted
whales and other marine mammals seasonally,
in spring gathered sea bird eggs, and in summer
harvested berries and edible plants. They made
clothing from hides, gut, and fish skins. Animal
bones were hewn into arrows, needles, and
fish hooks. Stones were hollowed into oil
lamps, and seal or whale oil was burned for
light or heat.

The Northwest Coast Indians of Southeast
Alaska and Northern Canada (Tlingit, Haida,
and Tsimshian) enjoyed a moderate climate and
settled in permanent villages. They gathered the
plentiful salmon, herring, deer, shellfish, and
edible plants. They made clothing from skins,
feathers, cedar bark, and mountain goat hair.
Rocks were fashioned into hammers and spear-
heads. Bark, roots, and grasses were woven into
useful baskets.

In the subsistence way of life, all nature's
offerings find a use and nothing goes to waste.

BRIDGET MANNION

Independent Spirit

In 1892, Irish immigrant Bridget Mannion was working as a cook for the wealthy Weare family in Chicago. One night, John J. Healy, an Alaska trader, and his wife Bella were dining at the Weares' house. Healy discussed with Weare the possibility of financing a trading post on the Yukon River near the new gold rush town of Forty Mile. When Weare agreed to finance the post, Bridget became determined to go North herself.

"But you can't mine," Mr. Weare protested.

"That's true," Bridget answered, "but there's them that can."

▼ Bridget Mannion (center), c. 1910, with relatives Katharine and James Hatchell (left) in front of the Hatchell's house in Seattle; Bridget and her husband lived down the street.

Willing to do anything to get to Alaska, she persuaded the Healys to offer her a one-year contract to serve as Mrs. Healy's maid. The party sailed from Seattle in the summer of 1892. In September they boarded a steamer at St. Michael for the trip up the Yukon River. But they were too late. The river was beginning to freeze, and Bridget and the Healys were forced to spend a cold winter at Nulato, site of one of the first Russian settlements on the Yukon River in Alaska's Interior.

In the summer of 1893 the Healys established Fort Cudahay across the river from the Forty Mile settlement. Bridget immediately embraced the frontier community, where there were few class distinctions. As one of the very few eligible woman in the region, she attracted countless suitors. True to her goal, she married a successful prospector, Frank Aylward, the first marriage in Forty Mile. As the wife of a wealthy

miner, she finally had enough money to visit her relatives in Ireland.

On her way to Europe she stopped in Chicago to see her former employer. Swishing into Mr. Weare's office in a silk dress, Bridget extended an elegantly gloved hand, saying, "Before I got fifty miles up the Yukon I had received 125 proposals of marriage, but held off until an engaging compatriot with a Kerry brogue and a mine that panned at a rate of $50,000 month, swore that he could not live without me. I am now on my way to Europe and I thought I'd like to see you as I went through."

Though Bridget lived in the North for only a few years, her bonds to Alaska were lifelong. She settled in Seattle, Washington, where she actively participated in the activities of the Yukon Order of Pioneers. She returned to Ireland in 1948, where she died ten years later at the age of 92.

YUKON RIVER TRADING POSTS

The Yukon River, Alaska's largest river, flows 2,000 miles from its headwaters near the Chilkoot Pass in British Columbia's coastal mountains in a northerly arc across the vast expanse of Alaska's Interior, then west to empty into the Bering Sea. Although much of the coast of Alaska had been charted by early explorers when the United States purchased the territory in 1867, few visitors had ventured up the rivers into the Interior by the 1880s.

In the early 1880s, Arthur Harper, Alfred Mayo, and Jack McQuesten, together with their Athabascan wives, established posts at sites along the Yukon River where nearby Natives could bring the furs they trapped to trade for goods. Each post consisted of a group of rough log structures, usually a large warehouse, a store, a cabin, and outbuildings, hastily built in a clearing along the river. During the gold rush years, these posts often became the center of new Native settlements. The populations at the posts also swelled when miners came in from the creeks for the winter, creating a demand for saloons, theaters, steam baths, lending libraries, laundries, and boarding houses.

While the Russians traded basic goods like beads, iron pots, steel needles, knives, and tea, the British brought in Hudson's Bay blankets and rifles. The Americans ferried even more goods upriver in small sternwheel riverboats, bringing more rifles and blankets, but also boots, calico fabric, and foodstuffs like dried beans, bacon, flour, sugar, coffee, and dried fruit. Prospectors depended on the posts for tools, ax heads, picks and shovels, and saw blades.

EMILIE FORTIN TREMBLAY   1870–1949

Young and in Love

After hiking over the Chilkoot Pass and rafting down the Yukon River, newlywed Emilie Fortin Tremblay arrived at the settlement of Forty Mile in June 1894. Still ahead was the sixty-mile journey to her husband Jack's claim on Miller Creek.

French Canadian Emilie was one of the first white women to come North as the wife of a miner. She had been living with her family in New York when she met fellow countryman Pierre–Nolesque Tremblay, known in the North simply as "Jack." Jack had been prospecting in the North since 1888 and had "struck it rich" as the owner of one of the best claims on the Sixtymile River. Most likely the nature of his trip Outside that fall of 1893 was to look for a wife. Emilie was twenty-three and Jack thirty-four when she agreed to accompany him to the Yukon.

Emilie's first home was spartan. Like most miners' cabins, it was crudely constructed of logs. Light came

▼ *Emilie Tremblay in front of the cabin where she spent a lonely winter in 1894–95. She was the only woman on Miller Creek, sixty miles from the town of Forty Mile. The new glass-paned window is an improvement over the original one made of bottles.*

EMILIE FORTIN
TREMBLAY

1870–1949

▲ *Early miners
shovel gold-bearing
gravel from the
creek bed into the
sluice boxes.*

through a single window made of bottles chinked together with mud. Her first task was to thoroughly clean the cabin, starting at the center pole which was covered by thick black residue spit by men who habitually indulged in chewing tobacco.

Although there were other women nearby in the town of Forty Mile, Emilie was one of only a few women on the creeks and the only woman for miles in any direction. She was further isolated because she spoke only French. She ate a miner's diet of beans—three times a day—accompanied by sourdough bread, sardines, or dried potatoes. Despite the time of year and the shortage of food, Emilie managed to put together a Christmas feast for the many miners living near the Tremblay cabin. She prepared roast stuffed rabbit, caribou, brown beans in broth, potatoes, and plum pudding with blueberry sauce, all of which she cooked on or in her small woodstove.

When the creeks finally thawed out and the spring rains came, Jack and Emilie washed out enough gold to visit New York. They later mined successfully on Eldorado and Bonanza Creeks in the Klondike, making enough for a comfortable life and even a trip to Paris. The Tremblays moved to Dawson City in 1914 when Jack's health began to fail. Emilie opened Madame Tremblay's, a small variety store, in a building that still stands in Dawson.

Difficult and lonely as that first winter on Miller Creek must have been, Emilie insisted her first year in the North was the happiest of her life.

Gold Rush Childhood

▲ *Crystal Snow grew up on the stage, entertaining miners in Juneau, Forty Mile, and Circle City. As a young woman, she studied music and pursued a professional singing career.*

Crystal Brilliant Snow was the gold rush daughter of veteran goldseekers in a theatrical family. Her father George and mother Anna met in a gold camp in California and later gave dramatic performances around the Northwest. When George heard rumors of gold in the Yukon Basin in 1887, he quickly accepted a six-week acting engagement in Alaska.

In Juneau, George found it more profitable to entertain miners than to join them prospecting for gold. The Snows brought the first legitimate theater to Alaska, presenting classical plays as an alternative to the town's bawdy dance halls and vaudeville shows. Three-year-old Crystal and five-year-old Monte sang for the miners, who would throw them gold nuggets in a show of appreciation. Since supplies came to Juneau only once a month by boat, Anna scrambled to sew costumes for each new show.

Over the years, George frequently left his family for long periods of time to prospect for gold in the Interior of Alaska. Crystal's mother eventually insisted the whole family accompany him. Their friends in Juneau thought they were crazy to go into such wild country, especially with children. But Crystal wasn't afraid. She was determined to prove that she could be one of the first little girls to climb the Chilkoot Pass.

In the spring of 1894, the Snows lashed their bedding, clothes, tools, a tent, and a year's supply of food to a Yukon sled and spent weeks on the trail ferrying their supplies up and over the pass. Every night at camp, Crystal and her brother helped out by cutting wood for the fire. Once over the summit, they walked along a series of frozen lakes until they reached the Yukon River. From there they traveled several hundred miles by boat to Forty Mile.

Life was easier in the new settlement. The family

**CRYSTAL
SNOW JENNE**

1884–1968

stayed with John and Bella Healy, old friends from Juneau, until their own cabin was built. Crystal and Monte went to school at the Buxton Mission run by Anglican Bishop William Bompas and Crystal learned to speak Athabascan. Her father was prospecting again, so she, her mother, and brother entertained the miners to support themselves.

Unable to stay put for long, George took off again in 1895 for the new gold strike near Circle City. When a broken collar bone prevented George from mining gold, the Snows built a log opera house and, once again, entertained the residents of a boom town. But the family soon left Circle City to follow the gold to the Klondike in 1896. They mined for gold all through that cold winter of 1897–98 and struck it rich at last.

The Snows left for Seattle in 1899, carrying more than $80,000. But Crystal's father lost it all when he poured all their money into a theater company that failed. The family ended up so poor that Crystal had to pawn her nugget necklace. The money was used to buy tickets for the family's boat trip back to Juneau.

Because she had so seldom attended regular classes, sixteen-year-old Crystal enrolled in school in Juneau as a fifth grader. Five years later Crystal was the only member of the second high school class to graduate in her beloved territory of Alaska.

Crystal became a professional singer and later a teacher. She married Dr. Jenne, a dentist, and raised three children in Juneau. She served two terms in the territorial house, only the second woman ever to do so, and she was Juneau's postmistress.

Crystal Snow Jenne died in Juneau at the age of eighty-four. Her life encompassed the changing of Alaska from an unexplored wilderness to the forty-ninth state in the union, a remarkable era.

▼ *Crystal Snow and her brother Monte were probably the only non-Native children in Forty Mile when they posed for traveling photographer Veazie Wilson in 1894.*

Chapter 2

KLONDIKE DISCOVERY

THE GREAT GOLD RUSH

By 1896, prospectors had been exploring the creeks and streams of the Yukon River Valley for nearly twenty years. Perhaps a thousand prospectors—including several women—were in the area. After the Forty Mile strike in Alaska, prospectors anticipated that the next discovery would be the "big one." But when George Carmack appeared at Bill McPhee's saloon in Forty Mile in August 1896 to announce what he had discovered on Rabbit Creek, a small tributary of the Klondike River in Canada's Yukon Territory, few of the experienced miners in the area paid any attention to him.

Carmack was not considered a serious prospector, and despite the fact that earlier deposits had been discovered by other Natives, local prospectors did not believe that his Athabascan relatives could recognize a promising claim. They'd been there, they said. The willow shrub slanted the wrong way; the landscape was not right. So most of the first claims in the Klondike were staked by newcomers.

Among the first to file claims on the creeks joining the Klondike River were two couples: Clarence and Ethel Berry, and Tom and Salome Lippy. They spent a grim winter sinking shafts to bedrock, but their efforts made them instantly rich. In the following spring when the river ice melted, wealthy Klondikers boarded the SS *Portland* and the SS *Excelsior* in St. Michael, bound for Seattle

◄◄◄ *The final ascent of the treacherous Chilkoot Pass, winter 1897-98.*

◄◄ *Clarence Berry always gave the credit to his wife, Ethel, for their success in the Klondike and later years. In 1898 Ethel (standing, right) looks on as Clarence examines the cleanup from the sluice box at their rich claims on Eldorado Creek.*

▲ *Mrs. Mizony, in front of her roadhouse where she cooked for gold seekers at Lake Bennett, 1898.*

and San Francisco. News of their discovery quickly captured international attention. Soon 100,000 adventurers, male and female, from all over the world and all walks of life, flocked North to the goldfields and the last frontier.

While extravagant lifestyles of the very wealthy at the turn of the century contributed to the image of the Gay Nineties, a financial panic in 1893 had actually left much of the nation impoverished. Men were thrown out of work, families evicted from their homes, and women reduced to picking wild berries to feed their hungry children. When the rush began, many people pooled resources, borrowed from friends and relatives, and set out on a quest they hoped would make them rich. And this time, women joined in the rush, wanting an equal share in the gold, inspired in part by the publicity generated by the roles of Ethel Berry and Salome Lippy in the discovery.

Business boomed as stampeders converged in Seattle, Vancouver, and San Francisco to outfit themselves. Most adventurers departed for the Klondike with little real information about the long journey ahead. To stave off the potential for mass starvation of the inexperienced travelers, Canadian authorities required the stampeders to bring with them 1,400 to 2,000 pounds of food, tools, and clothing—enough supplies for a year.

Two popular routes led most of the throng over the Coast Range and into the gold country. The traditional route was the steep thirty-two-mile Chilkoot Trail, which left from Dyea, a few miles along the waterfront from Skagway. An alternative route for pack horses was the forty-mile White Pass Trail from Skagway. The atmosphere in Dyea and Skagway was bedlam as crates of food, clothing, tents, and mining equipment were unloaded from the ships and dumped onto the mudflats and thousands of would-be stampeders tried to figure out which boxes were theirs.

Women with means, who had purchased the required "ton of goods," hired packers to haul their outfits over the passes. Other women arrived penniless and alone, but somehow managed to make their way, often carrying everything themselves in relays.

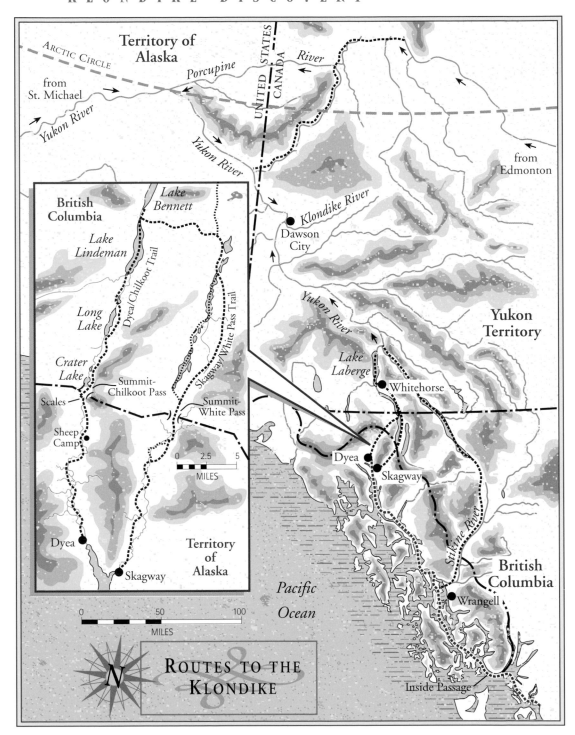

Territory of Alaska

ARCTIC CIRCLE

from St. Michael

Yukon River

Porcupine

Yukon River

River

UNITED STATES / CANADA

from Edmonton

Klondike River

Dawson City

Yukon River

Yukon Territory

Lake Laberge

Whitehorse

British Columbia

Lake Bennett

Lake Lindeman

Dyea/Chilkoot Trail

Long Lake

Skagway/White Pass Trail

Crater Lake

Summit-Chilkoot Pass

Scales

Summit-White Pass

Sheep Camp

Dyea

Skagway

Territory of Alaska

0   2.5   5
MILES

Dyea

Skagway

Stikine River

British Columbia

Wrangell

Pacific Ocean

0   50   100
MILES

Inside Passage

N

ROUTES TO THE KLONDIKE

Women soon discovered that in this land, how skilled you were wasn't as important as how prepared you were to handle adversity. Some women joined husbands and brothers to form the necessary numbers to pack their goods over the trail; others arranged to trade cooking in exchange for an escort or for packing their goods. Single women had to be resourceful and independent: sometimes a woman would be the only female working in a group of men unknown to her. In the Outside world, that situation was socially unacceptable, but in the Klondike it was a necessity. Embracing their new independence, women cut ties with their former lives.

Once over the passes, the hoards settled in a camp on the shores of Lake Bennett and built makeshift boats. When the spring thaw came, a huge flotilla of rag-tag craft drifted across the chain of lakes and floated down the Yukon River, darting through the Whitehorse and Five Finger Rapids. While some died and most people were scared to death, journalist Emma Kelly found the Whitehorse Rapids thrilling and walked back to raft the rapids again. The 800-mile float trip to the new boomtown of Dawson took the gold rushers anywhere from a few weeks to a few months.

While the Chilkoot and White Pass Trails were the most popular routes to the goldfields, eager and naive gold seekers were easy prey for promoters of other routes, too. Travelers over the 1,500-mile all-Canadian route from Edmonton, and those taking the difficult Stikine River route inland from Canada's Northwest Coast, among others, suffered even greater hardships, and most did not even get to the goldfields.

Some stampeders thought they could save themselves from crossing the high mountain passes and taking the long raft or boat trip downriver by traveling on steamships from Seattle to the Bering Sea coast village of St. Michael, and then going by sternwheeler to Dawson. Yet few who attempted this 4,200-mile journey made it to Dawson in 1897. Hundreds of travelers found themselves stranded for the winter of '97–98 at St. Michael, Rampart, or other settlements along the Yukon River because of freezeup.

Stampeders who finally reached Dawson almost two years after

George Carmack's 1896 discovery were disappointed to find that most of the claims were already taken. Homesick and broke, numbed by the hardships of the journey, thousands stayed on just to experience the carnival atmosphere of frontier Dawson, then sold their outfits and left before winter gripped the landscape once again.

Among those who stayed on were many women, buoyed by their new skills and experiences and intrigued by the many opportunities in this raw land. Their trip North had become a life-changing event. Stronger than they ever believed possible, they now became prime movers in this new way of life.

▲ *Navigating formidable Miles Canyon on the Yukon River near Whitehorse in a rough homemade scow was one of the dangerous challenges on the journey downriver to Dawson.*

KATE CARMACK

A Life Transformed

▲ *Shaaw Tláa, Kate Carmack, a Tagish Native, c. 1898, adorned with the Klondike gold she helped discover but which ultimately brought her much sorrow.*

Shaaw Tláa was a young woman when a small but steady stream of gold prospectors began to cross over the Chilkoot Pass and float down the lakes and rivers past the village of her Native Tagish people. The powerful Tlingit people who lived on the coast controlled trade over the Chilkoot Pass and arranged contracts of marriage to formalize trading partnerships with the Tagish. Shaaw Tláa, who was known as Kate, and her brother Keish (Skookum Jim) were among the eight children of one of these arranged marriages.

Kate was married to a Tlingit man and bore a daughter; both husband and child died. According to Tagish custom, Kate's mother then insisted she marry her deceased sister's husband, George Carmack, a prospector from California who had been living with his Tagish in-laws, packing goods on the Chilkoot trail with Kate's brother Skookum Jim and nephew Dawson Charlie. George and Kate were married according to Native custom and contract.

After a summer when both packed for William Ogilvie's 1887 exploration expedition, George and Kate set out to prospect along the Yukon River. For the next five years they prospected, trapped, and traded in the Fortymile and Stewart River areas. With Kate's skill and knowledge of the wilderness, they were able to live off the land. To support George's prospecting trips, Kate sewed mukluks and mittens to sell to other miners. Kate's niece, Kitty Smith,

KATE CARMACK

1867–1920

remarked, "He's got a wife, he's all right! She does everything, that Indian woman, you know, hunts, just like nothing, sets snares for rabbits. That's what they eat."

In January 1893 Kate gave birth to a daughter, Graphie Gracie, at a trading post they managed at the mouth of the Big Salmon River. In the spring of 1896, George, Kate, and Graphie Gracie set out downriver. At the same time, Kate's family, not knowing if Kate was alive or dead, sent Skookum Jim and Kate's cousin, Dawson Charlie, in search of her. They found Kate and George at the mouth of the Klondike River, a Native fishing site. There they encountered white prospector Robert Henderson who invited George to do a little prospecting with him on a promising creek. The group followed Henderson to his claim, but left when Henderson told them he didn't want "any Indians" to stake there.

▼ *Kate Carmack and her husband George and her daughter in front of their cabin on Bonanza Creek in 1898.*

▲ *Kate Carmack
never got any of the
money from the
Klondike gold she
helped discover. She
lived out her last
years in Carcross,
near the site of her
tribal village,
supported by a
pension from the
Yukon government
and money from
her brother
Skookum Jim.*

No one will ever know who actually discovered the gold that began the Klondike stampede. All participants claimed credit for it at one time or another. What is known is that George, knowing that a Native would not be allowed to register a claim, staked a discovery claim for himself on August 17, 1896, and gave one claim each to Jim and Charlie but Kate, a woman, got nothing.

George returned to Forty Mile to herald his find, carrying a rifle shell full of gold as proof of his find. Bartender Clarence Berry heard about the discovery, and went to search for himself. The rest is gold rush history.

Carmack's claims yielded hundreds of thousands of dollars in gold, making all three partners rich, but bringing sorrow as well. Kate and George traveled to the States along with other "Klondike Kings." Uncomfortable in the foreign environment and the glare of constant publicity that followed them, Kate began to drink heavily. At one point she was locked up in a Seattle jail as a public nuisance. The family went to live on George's sister's ranch in California.

George deserted Kate in 1900 and returned to Dawson. He eventually married Marguerite Laimee, a proprietor of a cigar store there. Marguerite insisted on erasing every mention of Kate from George's diaries, and George himself denied that he had ever been married to her. With the help of friends in California, Kate tried for several months to fight for her share of the gold. But because she was unfamiliar with the American legal system and had never married George under the white man's law, her efforts proved fruitless.

Desperately unhappy, Kate and Graphie returned to her people in Carcross, not far from the old village. Much had changed in her people's traditional way of life because of the Klondike gold rush, which she herself helped create.

George eventually lured Graphie to Seattle. The loss of her daughter was particularly troubling to Kate and her family, for by Tagish custom, a child belonged to her mother's clan. Kate died poor and unrecognized at the age of sixty-three during an influenza epidemic in 1920.

For a hundred years, Kate has not been given credit for her role in the Klondike discovery. But as the oral history of the gold rush from the Native people's point of view becomes part of the written record, Kate's contributions to the historic discovery are finally being recognized.

KLONDIKE DISCOVERY

While there are several versions of the discovery story, nearly everyone agrees that Kate and George Carmack, Skookum Jim, and Dawson Charlie were hunting for moose near Rabbit Creek when the fateful gold discovery took place. Some claim that George himself said it was Kate who first found the gold while he and her brothers napped after lunch. Wandering around, she found a bit of bedrock exposed, and taking a pan of dirt, washed it, and found that she had some four dollars in gold.

How do the Tagish people explain the Klondike discovery? According to legend, Kate Carmack's brother, Skookum Jim, had an encounter with Wealth Woman, a complex figure in Tagish mythology. Wealth Woman first appeared to Jim as a frog, which Jim helped to escape from a deep hole. Another time, while Skookum Jim and Dawson Charlie were camping on the shores of a lake at the summit of the Chilkoot Pass, they heard the sound of someone crying. It was Wealth Woman. But because they only heard Wealth Woman and didn't actually see her, they could not catch her. And so they believed the money they made from their gold discovery would not last. This certainly turned out to be true.

ETHEL BERRY

Bride of the Klondike

▲ Ethel Berry arrived in Seattle in 1897 as one of the first of the Klondike millionaires. She and her husband had less than $60 when she left California as a twenty-three-year-old bride just a year earlier.

Twenty-three year-old Ethel Berry, wearing a ragged housedress held together with a man's belt and shoes full of holes, stood on the deck of the steamer *Portland* as it tied up at the Seattle docks in July 1897. At her feet was a bedroll so heavy she couldn't lift it. Inside the bedroll was nearly $100,000 in gold. Ethel Bush Berry, a poor farm girl from Selma, California, was rich!

Pandemonium greeted the *Portland.* Newspaper headlines already heralded the arrival of the ship bearing its "ton of gold." Reporters covering the sensational story clamored to interview her. Ethel Berry's story, "The Bride of the Klondike," was featured in papers all over the world.

Asked what advice she would give to women who would go North, Ethel answered, "Why, to stay away, of course." But she added, "It's much better for a man, though, if he has a wife along. The men are not much at cooking up there, and that is the reason they suffer with stomach troubles, and as some say they did, with scurvy. After a man has worked hard all day in the diggings he doesn't feel much like cooking a nice meal when he goes to his cabin, cold, tired, and hungry, and finds no fire in the stove and all the food frozen."

Klondike Fever gripped the nation. Thousands of women saw an opportunity to make a fortune quickly. But none of them could imagine what Ethel's life in the North had really been like.

Just months before, Ethel had been huddled in a small wooden shack on Eldorado Creek with only a flour sack for a window. She panned the miners' paydirt by lamplight in a washtub that was also used for bathing. Outside, the rounded forms of the hills above, marked with the stubble of stunted trees, glowed in the dim dusk of the sun at noon in midwinter. Orange fires radiated near a hundred shafts sunk into the frozen

ground. Men, bundled in layers of rags, huddled near the flames and turned the windlasses that brought up the paydirt from the tunnels below. They piled the dirt on ever-growing "dumps," which Ethel and others sifted for gold.

When spring came, Ethel could pick up handfuls of nuggets off the claim. No one Outside yet knew of the discovery. The frozen Yukon River would not thaw until June, and until then, there was no escape from the Klondike.

Raised on a farm in the central valley of California, Ethel had married her childhood sweetheart Clarence J. Berry when he returned from his first trip to the Yukon in the fall of 1895. After a March wedding on her father's farm, Ethel prepared for a honeymoon trip over the Chilkoot Pass with a dog team and sleds.

"I put on my Alaskan uniform . . . the heavy flannels, warm dress with short skirt, moccasins, fur coat, cap and gloves, kept my shawl handy to roll up in case of storms, and was rolled in a full robe and bound to the sled, so when it rolled over I rolled with it and many tumbles in the snow I got that way," she reported.

After they arrived, Ethel spent two months alone in a tiny cabin in Forty Mile while Clarence worked out on the creeks. With no luck at prospecting, Clarence was tending bar in Bill McPhee's saloon in Forty Mile the August night George Carmack arrived to boast of his discovery at Bonanza Creek. The Berrys immediately headed for the new discovery and staked a claim on nearby Eldorado Creek; theirs would become one of the most valuable claims in the Klondike.

Ethel spent the winter of 1896–97 housekeeping, Klondike-style. "When I got there the house had no door, windows or floor, and I had to stand around outside until a hole was cut for me to get in. . . . We had all the camp-made furniture we needed, a bed and stove—a long, little sheet-iron affair, with two holes on top and a drum to bake in. The fire burns up and goes out if you turn your back on it for a minute. The water we used was all snow or ice, and had to be thawed. If any one wanted a drink, a chunk of ice had to be thawed and [the hot water] cooled again."

▲ *By the time the Klondike stampeders of 1898 arrived, the Berry claims on Eldorado Creek were well established and among the richest in the district. Their two-story cabin was the finest on the creek.*

The Berrys' Klondike claim became legendary. Despite the hardships of that first year, Ethel and Clarence returned to mine again in the spring of 1898. Ethel ascended the treacherous Chilkoot Pass a second time, this time with her sister Tot, amidst the chaos of thousands of gold rushers whose dreams of riches were inspired by her own story.

While many, if not most, of the "Klondike Kings" squandered their money, Clarence and Ethel Berry continued to work hard and invested their fortune wisely. They developed rich claims in Ester, Alaska, about nine miles west of Fairbanks. And beginning around 1907, the Berrys began a successful large-scale dredging operation in the Circle Mining District. For display at the 1909 Alaska Yukon Pacific Exposition in Seattle, Ethel loaned $70,000 worth of gold nuggets that she herself had picked up on their various gold claims. Clarence later sent the nuggets to Tiffany's to be fashioned into a dresser set.

Ethel, who in 1897 had declared she would never go North again, couldn't stay away. She traveled each year up the Yukon River by boat and by horse and wagon over Eagle Summit to visit their claims until her beloved Clarence died in 1930. The wealthy widow lived in Beverly Hills, California, until her own death in 1948.

KLONDIKE FOOD

*Stampeders were forced to unload their outfits on the beach at Dyea,
a scene of chaos and confusion.*

Within 48 hours of the *Portland's* arrival, [Seattle] was a bedlam. Money was dug out of safe-deposit boxes and flowed back into circulation. The streets were jammed day and night. In 90 days there came into our store the peoples of nearly every nation; men from Chile, Peru, South America, and Australia.

Queer lines of supplies came into being, everything possible was evaporated to reduce bulk. Plants in Seattle, Portland, and San Francisco made evaporated potatoes, reducing 100 pounds to 8 to 10 pounds, which sold at 20 cents a pound. Onions, evaporated in the same way, sold at 40 to 75 cents a pound. Yolks of eggs were placed in a large vat and by means of a belt turning were changed into a crystal form which sold at $1 a pound. One pound was equivalent to three dozen eggs."

—Isaac Cooper, owner of
    Cooper & Levy in Seattle, which
    outfitted many stampeders

"From actual experience I find evaporated eggs a failure. . . . The evaporated goods are a grand success. The onions, soup vegetables, and minced potatoes being especially palatable. The lists fail to mention butter, on account of its being looked upon as a luxury, but all the old Yukoners take in a goodly supply. Some carry the tub butter, while others prefer the two-pound tins. The miners say pure grease makes a pleasant drink. If so, butter will certainly not be amiss."

—Annie Hall Strong,
    The Skaguay News,
    December 31, 1897

HARRIET PULLEN

Civilizing the North

▲ *Harriet Pullen's personal sense of style established her hotel's reputation for elegance in the North, c. 1920.*

"When I first arrived in the North, I had only seven dollars to my name. I didn't know a soul in Alaska. I had no place to go. So I stood on the beach in the rain, while tented Skagway of 1897 shouted, cursed, shot, and surged about me."

Harriet Pullen may have been scared to death about her circumstances, but she was still able to recognize the opportunities a gold rush town offered. At five feet nine inches tall with a mass of dark red hair curled high on her head and wearing the latest fashions, Harriet cut an imposing figure. Her first job in Skagway was as a cook for Captain William Moore, one of Skagway's earliest settlers. Moore paid her three dollars a day to cook for the crews building the piers on Skagway's bustling waterfront. Since she had paid her own cook back home twenty dollars a month, her pay seemed like riches to her.

But Harriet soon found that three dollars did not go far food in a frontier town. She began making home-made apple pies using the surplus dried apples that were readily available, having been included in every stampeder's outfit. Harriet baked the pies in pie pans made from discarded tin cans and sold them for a handsome profit.

Taken by gold fever in the summer of 1897, Harriet had come North determined to make her fortune. Once well-to-do, her family's circumstances had changed. Seeing no opportunities in Washington state, she left behind her husband, daughter, and three sons and, on her arrival in Skagway, began her life anew, telling everyone she was a widow. With the money from the pies and her cooking, Harriet was eventually able to send for her sons, whom she believed were old enough to deal with lawless Skagway. And she sent for her horses, remnants of her once-privileged life.

As waves of gold seekers flooded Skagway, desperate

to get over the mountain passes to the goldfields, it became clear to Harriet that the big money was being made by the packers. Despite the disturbing stories she heard of suffering and dying pack animals on the White Pass Trail, she started a freighting business—one of only a few women ever to attempt to do so. Knowledgable about horses and conscientious about the care she gave them, her business thrived, making a profit of twenty-five dollars a day, more than enough to support her boys and to send for her daughter Mildred.

By July 1899 the White Pass and Yukon Route Railway was completed to Lake Bennett; a year later, the tracks reached Whitehorse. Where once horses and men had struggled and died, passengers could now travel in comparative comfort. All freighters were put out of business. Not one to sit on her heels, Harriet bought Captain Moore's grand house and converted it into the most memorable hotel in Alaska, the Pullen House.

Harriet's estranged husband traveled North to join the family, but after a time he disappeared over a pass into the Yukon and eventually returned to Washington's Olympic Peninsula. The Pullen House gained a reputation as a place of style and elegance. Harriet was frequently seen riding sidesaddle on her fine horse, or costumed in fringed and beaded Indian dress, entertaining her guests with gold rush tales.

She purchased the town site of Dyea and established a farm, providing her guests with homegrown vegetables and fresh cream—delicacies in the North. Her tables were set with fine linens, china and silver; the rooms were equipped with soft beds and bathtubs, a luxury in those days.

As quickly as it boomed, Skagway's exuberance waned after the stampede passed. Still, the Pullen House remained a civilized haven for weary travelers. Over the years Harriet collected enough artifacts to have her own gold rush museum, and until her final days, she continued to meet every ship docking in town. "Ma Pullen," as she was affectionately called, died in 1947 and was buried near the site of her once-vibrant hotel.

▼ *Harriet frequently dressed in Native costume to tell stories to her hotel guests.*

MOLLIE WALSH BARTLETT   1872–1902

The Angel of White Pass Trail

▲ *Mollie Walsh, an engaging young Irishwoman, ran restaurants in gold country and was extremely popular among her patrons.*

On the cruel White Pass Trail at the height of the gold rush in the spring of 1898, the sight of a diminutive Irish girl with long dark hair busily cooking in a forlorn tent must have seemed like a heavenly vision. Mollie Walsh endeared herself to worn-out travelers and overworked packers by offering compassion and home-cooked meals. Tragically, her life ended only four short years later.

A bright and industrious young woman, Mollie led a quiet life in St. Paul, Minnesota, working as a stenographer in her Irish American neighborhood. But in 1890 she ran off with a friend to Butte, Montana, one of the wildest mining towns in the West. And when word of the gold discoveries in the Klondike reached the miners in Butte in 1897, many eagerly set out for Dawson, including Mollie.

After her arrival in Skagway, Mollie got a job in one of Skagway's nineteen restaurants. She also became active in the church of the Reverend Robert M. Dickey, whom she had met on the boat coming north: churchgoing was a respectable activity for a single woman.

Mollie soon risked her reputation when she came to the aid of a dying prostitute, a girl she had gone to school with back home in St. Paul. As a favor to Mollie, Reverend Dickey risked scandal by holding the prostitute's funeral in his church. During the service, he urged the dead girl's compatriots to quit the profession. In attendance was a sea captain who was so moved by Reverend Dickey's speech, he offered free transport to Seattle for any prostitute wishing to leave. Money was raised to provide funds for the girls to make a fresh start elsewhere. Many of them accepted the offer, and left on the SS *Shamrock* that very night.

Prostitution was a valuable source of income for Soapy Smith and his gang of henchmen—pimps,

murderers, thieves, extortionists—who controlled Skagway through a network of criminal activity. Having frustrated the designs of Smith's gang and no longer able to abide their corruption, Mollie decided it was time to leave town. In March 1898, she bought restaurant supplies and paid Jack Newman to transport them thirty miles up the White Pass Trail into Canadian territory. Here, just beyond the summit and under the watchful eye of the Northwest Mounted Police, Mollie opened her grub tent, serving freighters like Harriet Pullen as well as the gold stampeders.

Well-known pioneer Sourdough Jim Pitcher recalled: "She operated a very primitive eating place with only a small sheet-iron stove and a narrow lunch counter in front of it. The eats weren't anything special, but the girl's hearty enthusiasm, quick wit, and a dusting of freckles made her a favorite with all who stopped there."

Mollie soon had her share of suitors, including "Packer Jack" Newman. But she was more attracted to Mike Bartlett, whose packing business had already made a fortune. By spring 1898 most gold rush stampeders had already passed through and the railroad to Lake Bennett was almost complete, putting many out of business.

Mollie abandoned her grub tent in June and headed for Dawson, where she opened another restaurant. In December she and Mike Bartlett were married. The next summer, Mollie spent time in Seattle enjoying her new prosperity, while Mike joined thousands of others looking for opportunities in Nome. Their son was born on the riverboat *Seattle #3* as the couple returned to Dawson in the fall of 1900.

Life should have been good, but by now the Bartlett brothers' fortunes faltered. Mike began to gamble and drink. The marriage soured and Mollie left her husband, taking her thirteen-month-old son, and accompanied by another man, John F. Lynch. Mollie and Lynch took a considerable amount of Mike Bartlett's money with them as well.

In a rage, Mike pursued them, following Mollie and Lynch to Seattle, Portland, San Francisco, even to Mexico. He finally caught up with them in March 1902 in Seattle. When Mike threatened to

▲ Proprietors and
travelers stand in
front of the Caribou
Hotel in Dominion
Creek, a large two-
story log structure
chinked with moss.
The hotel served as
a transfer station
for the Bartlett
Brothers' Packing
Company.

kill himself if Mollie didn't return to him, Mollie agreed to reconcile. Mike returned to Dawson to wrap up business matters, but when he rejoined Mollie in Seattle, his drinking worsened.

Mollie asked the police to arrest him, stating that he had "abused her in all ways and threatened to do away with her," but soon withdrew her complaint—a fatal error. A week later, Mike chased Mollie down a Seattle alley and shot her in the back.

After a costly and very public trial, Mike was acquitted of murder by reason of insanity and was sentenced to an asylum. Soon after his release, he hung himself. Mike's nephew was to create another chapter in Alaska's history when he became U.S. Senator E. L. "Bob" Bartlett, Alaska's first senator.

Mollie's story would have been forgotten were it not for "Packer Jack" Newman. Still in love with her, Packer commissioned a bust of Mollie that today stands in Mollie Walsh Park in Skagway with this inscription: "Alone and with help this courageous girl ran a grub tent near Log Cabin during the Gold Rush of 1897–1898. She fed and lodged the wildest gold-crazed men. Generations shall surely know this inspiring spirit. Murdered October 27, 1902."

Women have made up their minds to go to the Klondike, so there is no use trying to discourage them . . . our wills are strong and courage unfailing. There are a few things, however, a woman should carefully consider before starting out on this really perilous journey.

First of all, delicate women have no right attempting the trip. It means utter collapse. Those who love luxury, comfort, and ease would better remain at home. It takes strong, healthy, courageous women to stand the terrible hardships that must necessarily be endured.

The following suggestions may be of some value to those who are contemplating making the trip next spring. My experience thus far has shown me the necessity of women being properly clothed and equipped for the trip to the Interior, and I can speak with some assurance, having been especially observant along this line. First and most important of all, by far, to be considered is the selection of footwear.

It is not necessary to have shoes two or three sizes larger than one's actual last, simply because you are going on a trip to the Klondike. Get a shoe that fits, and if the sole is not very heavy, have an extra one added. The list that follows is the very least a woman should start with:

1 pair house slippers
1 pair knitted slippers
1 pair heavy-soled walking shoes
1 pair arctics
1 pair felt boots
1 pair German socks
1 pair heavy gum boots
3 pair heavy all-wool stockings
3 pair summer stockings
Moccasins can be purchased here of the Indians. The tall bicycle shoe with extra sole would make an excellent walking shoe. In the way of wearing apparel a woman can comfortably get along with:
1 good dress
1 suit heavy Mackinaw, waist, and bloomers
1 summer suit
3 short skirts of heavy duck or denim, to wear over bloomers

3 suits winter underwear
3 suits summer underwear
1 chamois undervest
1 long sack nightdress, made of eiderdown or flannel
1 cotton nightdress
2 pair arctic mittens
1 pair heavy wool gloves
1 cap
1 arctic hood
1 hat with brim broad enough to hold the mosquito netting away from the face
1 summer dress
3 aprons
2 wrappers
2 shirtwaists
snow glasses
Some sort of gloves for summer wear, to protect the hands from mosquitoes.

BEDDING
1 piece canvas, 5x14 feet
1 rubber blanket
2 or better 4 pair all-wool blankets
1 feather pillow
A ready-sewed tick will be very nice to have, for it can be filled with dried moss and makes a good pioneer mattress.

An old miner would no doubt laugh me to scorn for suggesting a little satchel or handbag, but the comfort derived from the hundred and one little extras a woman can deftly stow away in it will doubly repay the bother of carrying it."

—Annie Hall Strong,
The Skaguay News,
December 31, 1897

LUCILLE HUNTER

Another Kind
of White Person

▼ *African-American Lucille Hunter was raised in the Deep South, and had gone to work in the fields when she was thirteen. By the time this rare 1969 photo was taken in her tiny dwelling in Whitehorse with the crates and the painted gold pan, she was blind. She died about three years later at the age of 94.*

Lucille Hunter was only nineteen in the fall of 1897 when she and her husband Charles headed north to the Klondike gold-fields. Little is known about Lucille, but her presence in the North was remarkable for two reasons: she and her husband were among a handful of African American stampeders who came to the Klondike, and Lucille was nine months pregnant at the time of her journey.

The Hunters and thousands of others chose the Stikine River route to the Klondike, one of the most difficult ways to get there. The trail left from Wrangell in Southeast Alaska and followed the powerful

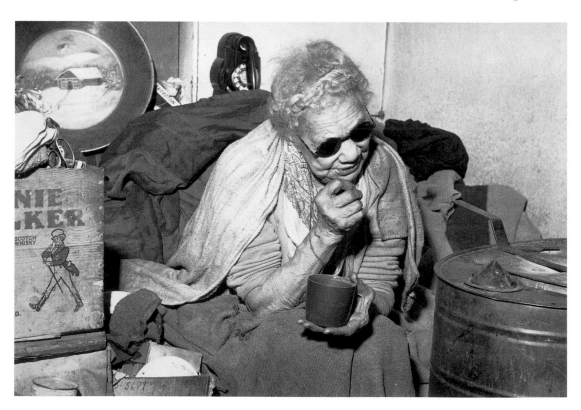

Stikine River through the snowcapped coastal mountains. The route up the river as winter approached was treacherous, but even more difficult were the 150 miles of rugged, almost impassable trail from the river overland to the goldfields. Almost all the stampeders complained bitterly about the conditions on the trail. Yet Lucille Hunter managed to keep up despite the fact she was about to have a child.

Lucille stopped only long enough at Teslin Lake to give birth to a daughter, whom she named Teslin, after the Tagish community. Most of their fellow stampeders stayed there for the winter. They built boats, and waited for spring breakup when they would float down the Teslin River to its junction with the Yukon. For the local Native people, the hoard of white prospectors in their midst was an unusual sight, but never before had they seen a black person. Not quite sure what to call the Hunters among all the white stampeders, the Natives simply described them as "just another kind of white person."

Charles and Lucille decided to press on alone, traveling by dog team, and arrived in Dawson after just after Christmas 1897. Charles may have had experience as a trapper or miner, to undertake this journey in winter. Without such northern survival skills, the Hunters surely would have perished in the –60° temperatures, deep snow drifts, and hundreds of miles of wilderness. They staked their claim on Bonanza Creek in February of 1898, well before the main hoard of stampeders arrived.

Lucille and Charles raised their daughter on the creeks around Dawson. After Charles's death in the early 1930s, Lucille continued to operate three gold claims in Dawson and a silver claim near Mayo. As Lucille did not own a car and did all the representation work herself, every year she walked the 140 miles from Mayo to Dawson and back again.

When most of the mines shut down during World War II, Lucille moved to Whitehorse, where she remained for the rest of her life. She lived in a small house in the middle of town and operated a laundry. Lucille died in 1972 at the age of ninety-four.

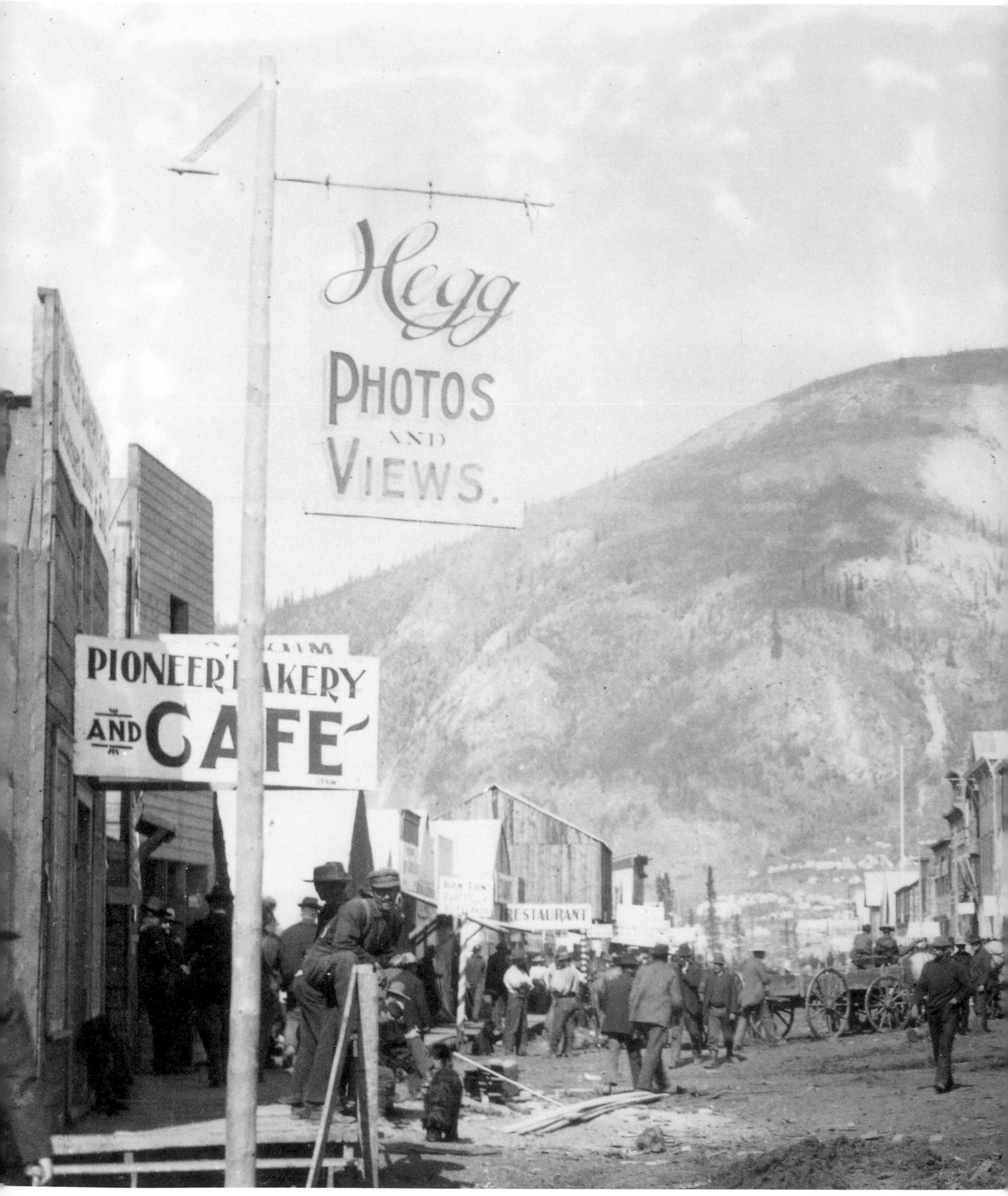
Hegg
PHOTOS AND VIEWS.
PIONEER
AND CAFE

Chapter 3

DAWSON CITY

OPPORTUNITY KNOCKS

Weary stampeders, having traveled hundreds of miles over harsh trails and rough waters, finally arrived at their destination at the confluence of the Klondike and Yukon Rivers: Dawson, Queen City of the Klondike goldfields. In the spring and summer of 1898, at the height of the Klondike stampede, Dawson bulged with miners. Newcomers quickly learned that most of the land had already been staked. And when it became clear that mining gold would not be simply a matter of plucking nuggets from the ground, many turned around and left empty-handed.

Dawson was a roaring mining camp. One prospector wrote, "The gambling and dance houses are thronged and the bars well patronized at all hours of day and night. Everything is topsy-turvy here. People are up most of the night and sleep during the day." There were limitless opportunities for hard-working women, who soon helped make Dawson more than just a short-lived boomtown. They cooked for the restaurants in town, built fancy hotels, entertained the miners, and ran their own mining operations. Unlike the lawless towns of Skagway and Dyea, Dawson's activities were constantly monitored by the Royal Canadian Mounted Police. Prostitution was tolerated as a necessary social evil and regulated. Alcohol, breweries, saloons, and gambling houses were taxed.

◄◄◄ *After a 1,000-mile trip through the wilderness, Dawson City in 1898-99 was a startling but welcome site.*

◄◄ *Belinda Mulrooney personally supervised the transportation of the fancy materials for her Fairview Hotel (in Dawson) over the Chilkoot Trail in 1898.*

▲ *The Kelly family and friends at their cabin at 21 Below Dominion Creek in 1901.*

DAWSON CITY

In February 1899 the White Pass and Yukon Route railroad tracks reached the White Pass summit. By summer, elaborately furnished steamships met railroad passengers at Whitehorse for the trip down the Yukon, helping to relieve the agonies endured on the trail.

With transportation no longer an obstacle, more middle-class women arrived in town, starting businesses and establishing hospitals, schools, and churches. Dawson began to take on a different character. The standards of morality for these women did not include socializing with the female entertainers, and certainly not the prostitutes.

In April 1899 a dance hall girl's upstairs room caught fire. Front Street, a hodgepodge of flimsy frame buildings insulated with sawdust, quickly went up in flames. Half of Dawson was destroyed by heat so intense that it melted the gold in the bank vault. The new Dawson, erected in the ashes of the old, was a more sophisticated town with a moral conscience to go with its new look.

▼ Pack trains transported goods and supplies to the mines on the creeks outside of Dawson in 1899, and returned loaded with gold.

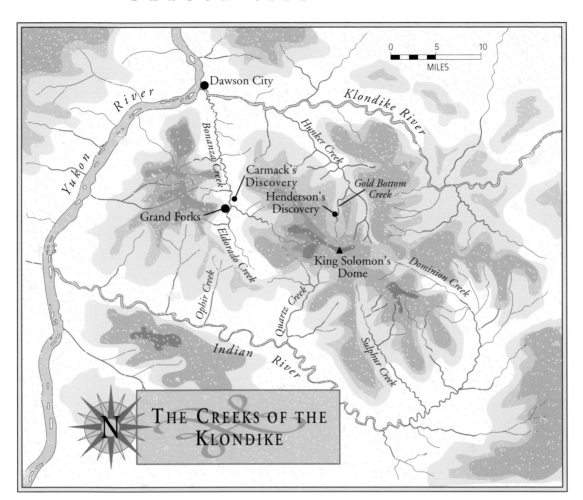

THE CREEKS OF THE KLONDIKE

When word of a big gold strike in Nome, on Alaska's Bering Sea Coast, filtered to Dawson, thousands of miners, convinced riches could be obtained faster there, left the Klondike. But many stayed, interested in the long-term mining possibilities and the advantages of living in an established town.

On the bright side, many of the worst characters had gone on to Nome and thus by September 1900 the authorities believed they had "stamped out" vice. Women, whether they stayed in Dawson or moved on, continued to enjoy unparalleled opportunities in the North and most had no intention of ever going home again.

BELINDA MULROONEY

Klondike Entrepreneur

▲ *A happy Mrs. Belinda Mulrooney Carbonneau at Atlantic City, New Jersey, c. 1900–1904.*

As the main hoard of stampeders made their way over the passes to the Yukon River in the spring of 1898, plucky Belinda Mulrooney was making her way over the Chilkoot Pass for a second time. But she was not looking for gold—at least not the kind that comes out of the ground. This time she was accompanying a shipment of expensive materials and fancy furnishings for the hotel she was building in Dawson, knowing it would likely not arrive safely without her.

Belinda had signed a contract with packer Joe Brooks in Skagway, paying him $4,000 to ferry her goods over the pass. Brooks, looking for easy money and figuring a woman wouldn't be hard to cheat, dumped her freight on the trail. Furious, Belinda immediately returned to Skagway and seized Brooks' pack train, retrieved her goods, and arrived in Lake Bennett riding Brooks' own horse!

Born in Ireland, Belinda grew up in Pennsylvania, the daughter of a coal miner. She left home in 1890 at age eighteen and two years later opened a restaurant at the Chicago Exposition. By 1896, she was in Juneau, a mining town in Southeast Alaska, where she managed a women's clothing store. When word of the gold discovery filtered out of the Klondike, Belinda invested in "silk goods and hot water bottles," and set out for Dawson.

Legend has it that when she arrived in Dawson in spring 1897, she threw her last half dollar into the Yukon River, vowing she would soon be wealthy enough not to miss it. Indeed, Belinda sold all her goods for a huge profit, which she used to finance her new ventures.

For women who provided a semblance of home—a warm meal and a clean bed—there was money to be made in the mining camps. Belinda built her first hotel at Grand Forks, where the fabulously gold-rich

Eldorado Creek met Bonanza Creek, about fifteen miles from Dawson and near Ethel and Clarence Berry's claims. The Grand Forks Hotel was an immediate success. While taking in money across the hotel's bar, Belinda heard men discuss who was selling mining claims and which claims were most valuable. She invested accordingly, increasing her growing fortune. All this she accomplished in 1897, and the main rush to the Klondike had hardly begun.

As Dawson swelled with new wealth, Belinda opened a second hotel, the Fairview, to rave reviews on July 27, 1898. Cut-glass chandeliers sparkled, tables were set with linen and silver, the thirty guest rooms, though small, were furnished with brass bedsteads. Rooms rates were $6.50 per night, meals $5 extra. The bar alone took in $6,000 the first day of business. Belinda hired a manager from Los Angeles and a chef from a famous restaurant in San Francisco, and the hotel flourished.

A born entrepreneur, Belinda next started a telephone company for Dawson and Grand Forks and a water company in Dawson. By 1900 Belinda was the most famous woman in the Klondike and one of its most successful business people. All she was lacking, it seemed, was love, though she had many suitors.

In stepped Charles Eugene Carbonneau, a Quebec champagne salesman who styled himself as a count and dressed accordingly in kid gloves, spats, and monocle. He wooed Belinda with red roses and flattering half-truths. They married on October 1, 1900, an event that was a social sensation in Dawson. The happy couple left for an extended fairy-tale honeymoon in Paris, where they paraded up and down the Champs Elysée in a coach drawn by white horses, their lives a whirl of champagne and fancy balls.

The couple spent winters in Paris and summers in Dawson, managing Belinda's mining and business interests. After a couple of years, Belinda's businesses began to falter and her money to evaporate, so she took over managing the mining properties herself. In 1904 after being indicted on charges of embezzlement, Carbonneau skipped Dawson with Belinda's furs and jewels, never to return.

▲ *Belinda Mulrooney
established the Dome
City Bank in the
Tanana District of
Alaska with her sister
Margaret in 1904.*

Carbonneau left behind a tangle of litigation. Her resources depleted, Belinda saw the new gold strike in Fairbanks as a chance to start fresh. She boarded the last boat out of Dawson in the fall of 1904, and within a month had options for claims on three of the richest creeks in the district—Cleary, Fairbanks, and Pedro. Belinda prospected and mined through the summer of 1905, left for the winter, then returned six months later with two of her younger sisters, Margaret and Nellie. The three women set up housekeeping in Dome City, a mining camp sixteen miles from the roaring gold-rush town of Fairbanks.

In May 1906, Belinda opened the Dome City Bank with profits from her mining claims. She incorporated the bank in August, naming her sister Margaret and a man named Jesse Noble as partners. As miners brought in record clean-ups from the surrounding creeks, the bank prospered and Belinda made another fortune, but legal problems continued to hound her.

Perhaps in a ploy to get a hold on Belinda's fortune, Jesse Noble married her sister Nellie in January 1907. The marriage was over before the honeymoon. Belinda herself finalized the separation by heaving Noble's trunk out a window.

Belinda and Margaret left Dome City and the North for good in November 1908. Nellie stayed in Alaska and eventually remarried. Ironically, Jesse Noble became an honored member of Fairbanks's pioneer society, even had a street named after him, while Belinda's part in the area's history is nearly forgotten. As free-wheeling and daring as many men, Belinda was one of the great entrepreneurs of the North Country, making and losing several fortunes, always ready with a new scheme.

When she left the North, Belinda bought property in Yakima, Washington, and used her fortune to support her family. She built a beautiful mansion, a local landmark that came to be known as Mrs. Carbonneau's Castle. By the end of her life, her money had run out. She died in relative obscurity in Seattle in 1967, at the age of ninety-five.

Placer miners washed their winter dump through a primitive sluice box, hoping to find flakes of gold.

Prospecting requires only a few tools: a pick, a shovel, and a gold pan. Prospectors look for gold along streams, in exposed rock outcrops, and in shallow surface deposits. They shovel promising sands into their gold pan and twirl them around in such a way that the dirt and rock are washed away. Small nuggets and the pinhead-size flakes of "flour gold" are left behind.

When placer mining gets a little more complicated, miners use a rocker—a box that rocks to facilitate the movement of coarse gravel through it and the sifting out of gold nuggets. The beaches of Nome were covered with these crude devices.

Klondike miners dug shafts by hand straight down to bedrock, where they hoped to find gold deposits. Because the ground was frozen in winter, they built fires to thaw it, then dug until they reached frozen earth again. It was cold, numbing work. They would thaw and dig all winter, heaping huge piles of gravel. When spring came and running water was available, these piles would be sluiced, and the valuable "wash" collected with the aid of quicksilver.

Hard-rock mining involves deep tunneling into the heart of mountains, with drilling, blasting, and pick-and-shovel work. The ore must be crushed to retrieve the minerals. There is back-breaking toil in loading and hoisting ore to the surface. Large mining companies in Juneau and Fairbanks employed hundreds of miners who used heavy machinery to dig tunnels several stories deep.

MARTHA LOUISE MUNGER BLACK 1866–1957

First Lady of the Yukon

It was summer 1898. Thirty-two-year-old Martha Purdy stood on the dock in Seattle. Behind her crowds of people eagerly lined up to purchase their ton of supplies at the Cooper and Levy Company before boarding ships bound for gold rush territory. Crates were stacked everywhere and hundreds of people milled about, wrangling over accommodations. Martha Louise considered herself lucky to have a ticket on a decrepit ship headed for Skagway.

Just weeks before, she had been living the life of a wealthy Chicago society matron with two young sons. She and her husband of 10 years, Will Purdy, had heard about the gold strikes in the Klondike. Will was tired of his job and Martha was bored with the social rounds, so they decided to go to the Klondike. Martha's brother George Munger would accompany them. Her sons would stay behind with Grandma Munger in Kansas.

As she prepared to leave Seattle, Martha received a telegram from her husband. Will had gone to San Francisco to coordinate arrangements and was to join her, but now, according to the telegram, he was backing out. He would not be accompanying her North. For a proper woman like herself to consider such an

▼ *Martha Louise Black enjoyed hunting and the outdoors with her husband George. Though a city girl, she fell in love with the magic of the North on her first trip over the Chilkoot Trail in 1898.*

expedition without her husband was unthinkable, Martha knew. Yet, she was sure there was a fortune in gold awaiting in the Klondike and there was no future, she believed, in her marriage. Martha decided then and there to leave her husband. She persuaded her brother George to chaperone her, in spite of his misgivings.

The first shock this modest society matron experienced on her way North was the lack of privacy she had to endure. With all available space filled on the ship, she was forced to share a stateroom with a gambler and his female companion. The ship was filthy. Passengers danced, gambled, and caroused the entire seven days of the voyage.

Martha and George arrived in Skagway on July 1, 1898. They hired packers, paying them $900 to carry their several tons of gear and supplies over the summit. The party set out on the Chilkoot Trail on July 12. At Sheep Camp, about thirteen miles up the trail, the party came across the remains of the tragic April avalanche, which had buried more than fifty people. Warm summer weather had melted the snow, revealing the bodies of some of the victims. Melting snow also made travel up the trail more difficult; Native packers tried to stop those who attempted the trail on unstable snow.

Her uphill march was made even more uncomfortable by her impractical clothing. As was the the fashion of the day, Martha wore a tight corset, high-collared blouse, long skirt, and full bloomers. Nearing the summit, Martha twisted her ankle on the rugged trail and collapsed into tears. Impatiently George chided her. "For God's sake, Polly, buck up and be a man! Have some style and move on!"

When they reached the summit, worn out and chilled to the bone, George paid an exorbitant $5 for enough wood to build a fire to warm themselves. Then they tackled the trail to Lake Lindeman. "I had felt that I could make no greater effort in my life than the last of the upward climb [on the Chilkoot Trail]," she recalled, "but the last two miles into Lindeman was the most excruciating struggle of the whole trip. In my memory it will ever remain a hideous nightmare. The trail led through a scrub pine forest where we tripped over bare roots of trees that curled over and around rocks and boulders like great devil fishes."

From Lindeman they traveled by boat down the series of lakes to the Yukon River. It was spring and the wildflowers were blooming along the river banks, and it was here that Martha began her lifelong interest in Northern wildflowers. The night before they reached Dawson, their party camped at Excelsior Creek, which Martha helped name. She and George staked the placer claims that they planned to work in the spring.

But things turned sour by the time they reached Dawson. With no room in town, Martha and George rented a cabin in a less reputable part of town across the river, an area called Lousetown. Martha discovered that she was pregnant with her third child. Terror-stricken, she realized she could never hike out of the Yukon in her condition, especially with winter approaching. Bearing this unwanted child in a little cabin, far from civilization, frightened her. But she had no choice.

Martha Louise survived those six months of winter 1898 without milk, sugar, or butter. Accustomed to many friends and engagements back home, as a pregnant single woman she found herself shut out from the Dawson social scene.

In her cabin on January 31, 1899, Martha gave birth to a nine-pound son, Lyman. Lonely miners flocked around her to celebrate a new life in their cold, dreary town. But before she could even begin mining, her father arrived to escort his wayward daughter home. Martha reluctantly agreed to go with him and promised that she would stay in Kansas with her parents and her children if her claims did not pan out at least $10,000 the following year under George's care.

Back home, Martha relished being close to her young sons, but the double failure of her marriage and her trip to the Klondike overwhelmed her. The only thing that lifted her depression were thoughts of the North and the freedom and liberty that Yukon life had given her. When reports arrived in June 1900 that her claims had indeed been productive, Martha eagerly returned to Dawson and

soon became the proprietor of
a mining camp and sawmill
financed by the Mungers.

For a single woman, life in
a mining camp was inhos-
pitable at best and at times
downright hostile. Men often
refused to take orders from a
woman. When some of her
workers tried to sabotage her
equipment, Martha called in
the Mounties to investigate the
crime. She and her son Donald,
then only nine years old, had

to run the mill alone when the men quit in protest. Her determi-
nation won out: Martha Louise became a successful business-
woman, and was soon welcome in Dawson's social scene. She
ordered elaborate gowns from Paris to attend the many parties and
was flooded with marriage proposals.

In 1904 she married attorney George Black. She continued to
pursue a passion for Northern wildflowers and put together a display of 464 varieties of Yukon wildflowers which was exhibited at
the Alaska Yukon and Pacific Exposition in Seattle in 1909. When
George was appointed Commissioner of the Yukon Territory in
1911, Martha used her position to welcome Canadians from all
walks of life and all levels of society to their stately home.

George Black was elected to the Canadian Parliament after
World War I. In 1935 when he had to resign his position for
health reasons, Martha was asked to run in his place. She ran as an
Independent, explaining, "I represent no party, I represent the
people of the Yukon." At the age of seventy, she became the second
woman elected to the Canadian Parliament.

Of her Klondike adventure, she wrote in her autobiography
My Ninety Years, "What I wanted was not shelter and safety, but
liberty and opportunity." Martha died in Whitehorse in 1957.

*▲ Martha Louise
Black was a society
woman in Chicago
before venturing into
the Klondike. Here
she and her husband
George have tea on a
camping expedition
in the Yukon.*

KLONDIKE KATE ROCKWELL   1873–1957

Belle of the Yukon

▲ *Klondike Kate had these postcards of herself in 1900 made to distribute at the popular Sourdough reunions in the 1930s.*

A sultry beauty swept through the smoky hall of the Savoy Theater in Dawson City. She was dressed in a flowing white gown with sweeping train and trimmed in rhinestones and seed pearls, her soft arms glittered with diamonds. Her red hair seemed on fire, covered with a shiny tin crown fitted with fifty lighted candles. It was Christmas Eve 1899.

Kate Rockwell led the miners around the room in the Grand March and later entertained them with her famous flame dance, after which they threw nugget after nugget in appreciation. "Belle of the Yukon," they called her. All the miners adored her, including a hermit named John Matson, a miner who rarely came to town. But Kate loved only one man, Alexander Pantages, a new arrival in the Yukon from Greece.

Kathleen Eloise Rockwell was born in Kansas, the daughter of a railroad man and a waitress. She was raised by her mother and stepfather in Spokane, Washington. As a child, Kathleen entertained her friends with songs and jokes and often skipped school. She was so rebellious as a teenager that her parents sent her off to boarding school—where she was expelled.

Kathleen and her mother moved to New York when her mother divorced a second time. She tried to pursue her dream of becoming a show girl, but after months of hoofing it without much success, she took her dreams to the Klondike.

She arrived in Skagway in 1899, and rode the train to Lake Bennett. When a Mounty refused to let women ride the rapids on the Yukon River, legend has it that Kathleen dressed like a boy and jumped aboard a boat.

She determinedly made her way to Whitehorse, supporting herself with tap-dance performances at every settlement along the way. She was offered a job in Dawson by the Savoy Theatrical Company which, with 173 performers and a full orchestra, was the largest theater troupe to perform in the Klondike. Kathleen mesmerized the men she entertained. Her act was an instant hit and she became known as Klondike Kate.

As a dance hall "percentage girl," Kate danced with the miners after her performances, earning commissions on the drinks she sold. "My best night I earned $750, mostly just for talking to a lonesome miner," she said. Despite her innocent appearance, she was not above cheating men out of their money. With the help of her lover, Pantages, Kate plied weathly miners with drinks, while Pantages refilled the empty bottles with watered champagne. Kate resold the "champagne" to the inebriated customers.

Pantages soon persuaded Kate to leave the Savoy and bankroll a new theater with him. With Kate as headliner, the Orpheum opened in Dawson to receptive audiences. Flush with success, Pantages talked of his dream of owning a string of theaters across the country. Kate assumed they would accomplish this dream as husband and wife.

By 1902, with Dawson on the wane, the couple left the North. Pantages began buying up theaters around the Pacific Northwest and encouraged Kate to travel on her own to earn money for other theatrical enterprises. During one of Kate's road trips, Pantages, to Kate's astonishment, married a young violinist named Lois Mendenhall. The man she adored robbed Kate not only of love but also of her Klondike fortune, a betrayal from which she never fully recovered.

Although Kate continued to tour for some time, her rough and tumble years in Dawson had aged her. Eventually she moved to central Oregon and tried to start a new life, supporting herself by working odd jobs. While most other Klondike dance hall girls went on with their lives and often buried their past, Kate clung to her identity as the Belle of the Yukon. Passing out postcards and giving interviews, she traded on her dancing days whenever she could.

In 1929 Pantages was charged with attempted rape in a case that was highly publicized. Kate was brought in as a material witness for the prosecution. Though she was never called to the stand, she sat in the courtroom day after day, attracting much of the attention and conjecture in the sensational trial. Pantages was eventually found guilty.

Far away from the hubbub of the trial, a lonely hermit saw a picture in the newspaper of the beautiful dance hall girl he had adored thirty-one years ago. John Matson, still mining in the Yukon, wrote Kate and asked her to marry him. She accepted, perhaps eager for the publicity or for his money. Kate made the most of her new identity as the aging Klondike bride. She continued to live in Oregon and make public appearances during their marriage. John Matson remained alone in his Yukon cabin, where he died thirteen years later.

Kate spent most of her life playing the role of Klondike Kate. Fun-loving and eager to share the details of her notorious past, Kate kept the glory days of the Klondike alive until she died in 1957.

Klondike Kate in a dancing costume at the height of her career in Dawson City.

"Many good and virtuous girls, who came to Dawson to seek honest work in order to better their impoverished condition from the slavish position they held elsewhere, braved to little purpose the heart-rending dangers which they nobly conquered along the trails, for unable to obtain employment they drifted into one of the too numerous dance-halls, and thence to ruin and disgrace."

—Alice Rollins Crane
Dawson Daily News, January 1902

While every man could get a job at the business end of a number-two shovel, any woman with enough stamina qualified as a dance hall girl or "percentage girl" in entertainment establishments and saloons. For a dollar, a lonely miner could spend a few minutes whirling a woman around the dance floor of a saloon or gambling house. The women received forty or fifty dollars a week, plus a percentage on the drinks they sold. While the women on the dance floor wore the typically modest dress of the Victorian era, onstage dancers and variety girls like Klondike Kate wore more revealing costumes and after performing changed to fashionable Paris gowns to sell drinks.

With so much money to be made, popular actresses and performers followed the gold seekers to Dawson, such as singer Cad Wilson and vaudeville performer Violet Raymond.

Prostitutes arrived in Dawson as early as the first gold stampeders in 1896. Prostitution was certainly not condoned, but it was tolerated as a necessary social evil, and the Mounties regulated the trade. The Dawson Board of Health instituted medical controls and inspections to prevent the spread of disease.

Though prostitutes and dance hall girls were sometimes portrayed as lively and cheery, their fate often was more desperate. Their lives often ended in tragedy involving suicide, abuse, and sometimes murder.

A CLEAN UP No. 11 DEXTER

Chapter 4

BEYOND THE KLONDIKE

RAMPART AND NOME

When gold was found by John Minook in Alaska's Interior in 1896, the discovery could have sparked the greatest Northern rush of all. But the find was immediately eclipsed by the Klondike discoveries, which occurred about the same time. Nevertheless, Big and Little Minook Creeks were staked and there was enough action to create a new boomtown, Rampart.

At the heart of Rampart were Al and Margaret Mayo, the trader and his Athabascan wife. After twenty years moving up and down the Yukon, operating the various trading posts that supported the prospectors in the Yukon River Basin, they decided to settle permanently in Rampart. Many of their grown children joined them in Rampart, as did many of Margaret's Koyukon Athabascan relatives.

Rampart was an important stop for the Yukon River boats, and it was at the beginning of a trail system that led back through the hills to other gold creeks. Because Rampart supported a population of only about 1,500 during its peak years of 1898–99, the local Athabascans were able to continue their traditional way of life alongside the mines and miners. Eventually a mission, newspaper, and even a government agricultural station were established in the area, in addition to the mines.

In 1898, gold was found in the creeks amid the rolling

◄◄◄ *Rampart, Alaska, was established as a few rough cabins in a clearing on the banks of the Yukon River in 1897.*

◄◄ *Women from Nome frequently traveled out to the mines for "cleanup" (examining the sluice box yield) as on this occasion on Dexter Creek, c. 1906.*

▲ *Many enterprising women in the North made a good living offering food and shelter to cold and weary travelers.*

tundra-covered hills of the Seward Peninsula along Alaska's Bering Sea coast. Three men of Scandinavian descent, the "Three Lucky Swedes" as they were called, had been on their way to the Klondike fields, and had stopped to prospect in the Cape Nome area around the Snake River. Quite by accident they stumbled on one of the richest gold creeks of the North, Anvil Creek.

By the following spring, a few hundred men had staked 1,500 claims and Nome was established. Nearly 3,000 more stampeders arrived as soon as the ice broke up and navigation opened in early summer. Some of the stampeders had been trying to reach Dawson but had been stranded at St. Michael or on the Yukon River during the winter.

Stampeders deserted Dawson for the Nome strike and continued over the Yukon River ice throughout the fall and winter of 1899–1900. By the spring of 1900, 20,000 to 30,000 travelers left West Coast ports in every available craft and converged on Nome, which could be reached directly from Seattle by ship, without a day's travel on foot.

The city of Nome sprang from the tundra, growing from a collection of tents and driftwood shacks into one of the wildest, most lawless and dangerous boomtowns in North America. Unlike Dawson, Nome had no mounted police to keep order. It was not an atmosphere that was hospitable to women or conducive to community building. Some women carved out a place for themselves, but most saw it only as a place to get rich and planned to move on.

By 1906, most of the easy money had been made in Nome and many prospectors and miners moved on to Fairbanks. The creeks around Nome continued to yield gold for intrepid solo miners until about 1915, when large-scale corporations took over the ground from the independent miners. Although mining continues on a smaller scale in the Nome area, little is left today of the fabulous boomtown on the beach.

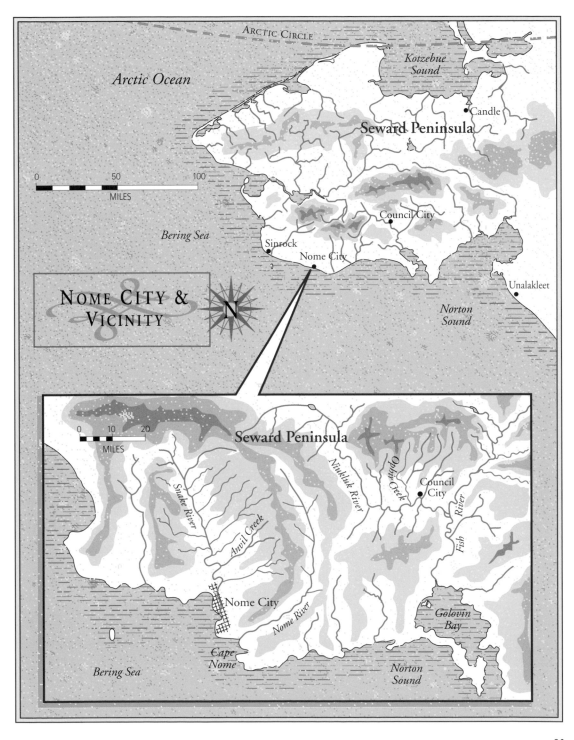

MARGARET MAYO

Matriarch of the Yukon

▲ *Stories of great-grandmother Margaret Mayo are told today by her many descendents in Alaska's Interior. She is widely remembered as a woman who adapted to changing times while maintaining her traditional Athabascan values.*

Of all the women who participated in the Northern gold rushes, none have been more persistently overlooked than the Native women. While the gold rush contributions of traders Arthur Harper, Al Mayo, and Jack McQuesten, who established posts along the Yukon River, are acknowledged, the very existence of their Athabascan wives is rarely mentioned in historical accounts. The stories of these women have been preserved only in family records and lore.

In 1874 fourteen-year-old Neehunilthonoh was among the first of her Native people to marry an American, trader Al Mayo. Neehunilthonoh, called Margaret, was the daughter of the chief at Nuklukayet, an important Native trading site. Like Kate McQuesten, Margaret was living at Kokrine's, a trading post thirty miles from Tanana, caring for storekeeper Kokrine's small son when she met Al Mayo, a gregarious twenty-seven-year-old former circus performer.

A few days after they met, Mayo asked Margaret's parents' permission to marry her. At first her family said no, because Margaret's mother knew that many white men eventually abandoned their Native wives. Before granting permission, she made Captain Mayo promise that he would always take care of Margaret. The couple was married according to Athabascan custom, and Al never broke his promise to Margaret's mother.

Over the next eight years, Al and Margaret operated the store at Tanana Station, along with Jennie Harper, Margaret's cousin, and Jennie's husband Arthur. Margaret bore five children at Tanana. After the Stewart River gold strikes in 1884, the Mayos moved the trading company to Fort Nelson, far up the Yukon River. During the trip, Margaret's sixth child was born prematurely and died.

Four years later in 1888 the Mayos moved to Forty Mile, along with the Harpers and McQuestens, following the new gold strikes. The three older Mayo boys were sent Outside to school in Wisconsin; the younger ones attended school at Buxton Mission. Margaret bore three more children in Forty Mile. In 1894 the family returned to Tanana Station, where Margaret had twins.

Al and Margaret did not follow the stampede when the big

Klondike strike came. They chose instead to open the Alaska Commercial Company trading post at Rampart, where they also operated a small hotel. Margaret's grown children and many of her Athabascan relatives joined them in Rampart.

The population of Rampart swelled during the winter of 1898–99, when boatloads of stampeders heading up the Yukon to the goldfields were stopped by ice and forced to winter over in town. Among these stampeders were Wyatt and Josephine Earp. Josephine visited with Margaret over the long winter.

To Josie, Margaret seemed very Americanized. She described Aggie Mayo as "a nice person ideally suited to her husband as she kept his house in the manner of a typical American housewife, tending a garden and reading books."

But Margaret was an important influence in the developing town, maintaining strong ties with her own people while establishing relations with newcomers. She successfully integrated the Native and white cultures, raising ten children at a time when disease and alcohol were killing many of her people. She was determined that her children receive an education, and she made sure her children were baptized in a church, yet she continued to practice many of her Native traditions. She maintained kinship ties with her relatives, supplemented her family's store-bought diet with fish and rabbit, and sewed fur clothing for her children. Futhermore, Margaret was well-respected as the town midwife.

Of the three original traders (Harper, Mayo, and McQuesten) Al Mayo was the only one to live out his days in the North with his wife by his side.

▼ *Margaret and Al Mayo and family, c. 1905. Thirteen-year-old Kitty (far left) was about to go Outside to school in San Francisco, 3,500 miles away. The other children (left to right) are Florence, seven, grandson Sullivan, and Antoinette and Annette, eleven-year-old twins.*

SINROCK MARY

Reindeer Queen

▲ *Mary Antisarlook, "Sinrock Mary," was the owner of a large reindeer herd, making her the wealthiest Russian-Eskimo woman on the Seward Peninsula. She was a popular figure in the Nome area when this postcard was made.*

In the winter of 1900 a group of miners of the Nome gold rush saw a solitary Eskimo woman driving a herd of reindeer across the frozen tundra, and followed her. The men desperately wanted the reindeer for food and to use as pack animals to haul supplies and equipment. The woman, known as Sinrock Mary, was a large, imposing figure with curly hair and a traditional Inupiat tattoo on her chin. She refused to stop for the miners. Again and again, the white prospectors called her names, trying to intimidate her. They shot at the herd to scatter the animals. They offered Mary liquor and some even proposed marriage in order to take control of her herd. Sinrock Mary held her ground. She had worked too hard to own and keep her herd and no man—white or otherwise—was going to take it from her.

Called Changunak, Mary was the daughter of a Russian trader and Inupiat Eskimo mother. She had grown up in the relatively cosmopolitan coastal village of St. Michael, a trading post on the Bering Sea, where foreign ships docked almost daily. Mary could speak several languages—Inupiaq, Russian, and English. Her mother taught her skin tanning and sewing, how to preserve edible plants, and how to share in the Eskimo way.

In 1889 Mary married Charlie Antisarlook, an Inupiat, and the couple moved to Cape Nome. Late in her life she told school children that "there were no people there [in Nome], not any groceries, either. Their food wasn't like what the Eskimos of St. Michael work hard [for wages] to have." For the first time, living far from a trading post store, Mary learned at Cape Nome how to live the traditional subsistence way, living on "real simple food, like whale meat, seal oil, rabbits, and ptarmigan."

After years of assisting with government reindeer herds, Mary and her husband became the first Alaska

G O L D   R U S H   W O M E N

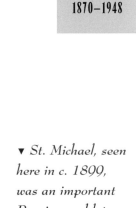
Natives granted their own reindeer. They moved with their herd to
Sinrock, a settlement near Cape Nome. After Charlie died in a
measles epidemic in 1900, Mary fought and won the right to own
half of the couple's 500 reindeer. By that time, news of the riches of
the newly discovered Cape Nome mining district brought 20,000
stampeders to the beaches of Nome. It was a spot where, a year earlier, there had been only a seasonal fishing camp.

Because all supplies had to be brought in from Outside, prices
were high. During the winters especially, any kind of fresh food
was at a premium. Sinrock Mary sold reindeer meat to the army
post, to the stores at St. Michael, and to miners working in the
area. Her herd made her the richest Native woman in the North,
and her fame grew.

The Inupiat Eskimos of the Seward Peninsula suffered greatly
with the arrival of the stampeders. Susceptible to diseases such as
influenza and mumps brought by white miners, entire families and
even whole villages fell sick and died. Because life as a Native
woman, and a single one at that, was so difficult in Nome, Sinrock
Mary moved her herd to Unalakleet in 1901 to get away from the
gold miners. The following year she married Andrew Andrewuk,
an Inupiat, who took no active interest in her herd.

Sinrock Mary continued to tend her reindeer herd for many
years. She trained Inupiat men as herders. And she stalwartly maintained her right to own her
herd, even though it was
asserted that as a Native and a
woman, she could not own
property. She adopted several
children, many of whom grew
up to be reindeer herders
with their own herds. Among
the Inupiat, Mary was known
for her generous spirit and
for sharing her wealth in the
Eskimo way.

▼ *St. Michael, seen
here in c. 1899,
was an important
Russian and later
American trading
post. Here goods
and people from
ocean steamers were
transferred to flat-
bottom river boats
for the trip up the
Yukon River.*

Boomtown Romantic

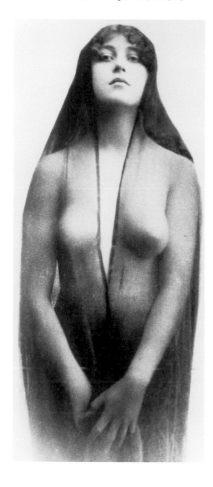

▲ *This photo of an actress in the 1880s has circulated for many years as a photo of Josephine Earp. Josie ran away from her San Francisco home at eighteen to join a traveling theater company. Later, to live down her notorious past, she may have destroyed all earlier photos of herself.*

In the late summer of 1898, Josephine Earp stepped off the SS *Brixom* in St. Michael after an exhausting trip from San Francisco. St. Michael, once just a small trading outpost of the Russian America Company, was the starting point for riverboat traffic up the Yukon River to the Klondike goldfields. The scene that greeted Josie at the waterfront was utterly chaotic. Hundreds of stampeders milled about, waiting for transfer to a boat for the 1,700-mile trip to Dawson.

Although Josie and her husband, Wyatt Earp, had managed to book passage upriver, other passengers who had paid for tickets were dismayed to find that their scheduled boat didn't even exist. She wrote, "They swarmed in a mob on the beach, as they begged and threatened, bribed and connived in every conceivable manner in trying to secure passage to Dawson."

The Earps waited nearly two weeks in St. Michael while their boat was being built. Unfortunately, by the time the boat made its way through the lower river delta, it was well into September. Winter would soon be upon them. "There was a frosty chill to the night air. Geese were moving south," she wrote. "The leaves of the trees and bushes along the shore had turned yellow and were falling. The landscape was growing bare. . . . The huge empty country captivated me. It was so big and awesomely quiet. Somehow it was different from the West—it seemed more remote and withdrawn. . . ."

Josie and Wyatt were boomers—members of an itinerant population of gamblers, saloon keepers, and camp followers who traveled from gold rush to gold rush. She and Wyatt would stay only as long as the camp boomed, then follow the action to the next boomtown. The couple shared "an insatiable desire to travel—to see new people and places."

GOLD RUSH WOMEN

The daughter of respectable German Jewish immigrant parents, Josie's upbringing was "all directed toward taking my place some day as a proper matron in a middle-class setting," she wrote. It was a path she rejected, opting instead to travel with a theater company.

Josie moved to Tombstone, Arizona, in the spring of 1880, and began a relationship with Wyatt Earp, the Western lawman. After his participation in the shootout at OK Corral, Josie and Wyatt spent a few years mining and prospecting in Colorado, Idaho, and Montana. They also followed the gamblers' circuit around Southwest mining boomtowns.

In 1897, hearing news of the Klondike gold strike, they set out from San Francisco, knowing little about what lay ahead. They took a boat to Skagway, heading for the White Pass Trail. But they got no farther than Juneau before thirty-five-year-old Josie discovered she was pregnant. The news provided them a reason to turn back. But Josie suffered a miscarriage, so the following summer, in 1898, they headed for Dawson once more, this time via the more comfortable all-water route through St. Michael.

By the time their steamer left St. Michael, slush-ice had begun to form on the Yukon. It became obvious that the Earps would not reach Dawson this time either, at least before winter.

Freezeup found them at Rampart, where Al and Margaret

◄ *The* Governor Pingree, *a typical sternwheel riverboat, was the craft on which the Earps traveled up the Yukon River in 1898.*

Mayo had established a trading post. With so many stranded stampeders and local mines yielding rich lodes, Rampart was a lively camp. The Earps rented a cabin belonging to gold rush writer Rex Beach for $100 per month. Josie fixed it up with calico curtains, fur robes for bedding, and burlap sacks for carpeting. The couple frequently dined out and enjoyed the company of a few old acquaintances from the gambling circuit in the West. Josie visited with Margaret Mayo, who found the time to make her a white fur parka.

After breakup in spring, Josie and Wyatt left Rampart. But instead of continuing on to Dawson, they returned to St. Michael to operate a canteen, selling beer and cigars. By late summer 1899, Wyatt decided the new boomtown of Nome was the place to be. When they arrived, Josie was amazed at the bedlam on the beach. "The town at the time was only a messy sprinkling of tents and half a dozen very rough lumber shacks."

Wyatt and his partner Charlie Hoxie immediately started building the Dexter Saloon, the first two-story structure in Nome. With no decent place to live for the winter, Josie and Wyatt decided to leave Alaska. They returned the next summer with thousands of dollars worth of fixtures and furnishings for the saloon, including thick carpets, fine mirrors, carved sideboards, and draperies. The Dexter became the most fashionable saloon in town, and the money rolled in. Old friends like John Clum and horse-racing partner Lucky Baldwin joined the Earps in this wild frontier town, and at first Josie enjoyed an active social life.

But during the long Northern winter, Josie suffered from depression, which she tried to cure by gambling. In the summer of 1901, after only a year in Nome, Josie and Wyatt had accumulated enough wealth from their Alaskan adventures to live well. After prospecting throughout Nevada, the couple opted for a quieter life, mining their desert claims in Parker, Arizona, and spending summers in Los Angeles. Wyatt died in 1928. Settling down to life as a respectable widow, Josie kept the memories of her wild youth private until her death in 1944.

BIRDS EYE VIEW OF NOME FROM LANE'S DERICK · 1903

*Goldseekers arriving in Nome after 1900 set up tents
on the beaches for ten miles in either direction.*

By 1899, those who had not struck it rich in Dawson headed for Nome. Latecomers arriving in the summer of 1900 were disappointed to find that all of the nearby creeks were already staked. Thousands of destitute people put up tents along the beachfront. They soon discovered that the very sands they were camped on were rich in gold:

they had stumbled upon a poor man's paradise.

It was widely believed—mistakenly—that the gold in the sand came from the depths of the ocean and was deposited onto the beach by the action of the waves. The beaches were crowded with humanity. Thousands of men, women, and children busily worked the beach with crudely made gold rockers.

FRANCES ELLA FITZ

Perseverance Pays Off

▲ *New Yorker Frances Fitz was a middle-class stenographer before traveling to Nome in 1900 to make her fortune.*

Frances Ella Fitz arrived in Nome along with thousands of other stampeders in the early spring of 1900, after traveling over 7,000 miles across the North American continent to seek her fortune. Fizzy, as she was known, had joined one of the many companies that had formed to invest in the gold rush: individuals would pool their resources to stake and develop large blocks of claims, and if the claims paid out (they rarely did), the investors would be rich.

Fizzy's company was controlled and directed by a man named Rowe, who had agreed to pay Fizzy's travel and investment expenses if she signed a contract to work as the company's secretary. Fizzy had no investment money of her own, and was thrilled for the opportunity to go North. Once in Nome, Fizzy lived in a tent on the beach like most of the stampeders. Because Rowe's company was not making a profit, she took a job with a law firm to support herself. That summer she worked day and night typing up claim notices, only to discover that the lawyers she worked for were in league with Arthur H. Noyes, a corrupt federal judge appointed to bring order to Nome's chaos. Unwittingly, Fizzy had become embroiled in one of the most notorious scandals of the gold rush era, that involved illegal claim jumping and more.

Horrified, she quit and went back to work for Rowe, honoring her contract with him, though she had yet to see any money. That winter, Rowe insisted that Fizzy join a party of several men who were going out to assess the company's claims around the small settlement of Roweburg, about eighty miles from Nome. Since the company couldn't afford to buy dogs, the men had to pull sleds loaded down with 500 pounds of mining supplies for the ten-day trip. It was a trip that would nearly cost Fizzy her life.

As the party set out, deep soft snow made travel slow and arduous. Pouring rain then turned snow to slush. The melting snow made it impossible to pull the sleds, and the party was forced to take shelter in a dismal little cabin. For seven long days they waited for the rain to stop, their food supply rapidly diminishing. When the rain stopped, temperatures of –40° returned.

Instead of heading straight for Roweburg, Fizzy and the group were sent to remote claims to perform yearly assessments, required by law, so that Rowe wouldn't lose ownership. When Fizzy finally arrived in Roweburg after a grueling fifty-two days, she had lost thirty pounds, having been severely burned in a campfire accident and stranded in a blizzard for seven days with no food. She spent that winter of 1900–1901 sleeping on a bunk made of spruce poles in a crude cabin in the wilderness, mediating among the warring factions of the company, all as furious as she was with the unscrupulous Rowe.

By spring Fizzy cut her ties with Rowe and found a job as deputy recorder of Council, also the home of Klondy and Alma Nelson. She soon saved enough money to buy a small cabin. Through her work in the recorder's office, Fizzy discovered valuable unstaked claims on Ophir Creek for which the yearly assessments hadn't been done. She filed them for herself.

As soon as she began to accumulate some money, Rowe appeared again at her side. He managed to convince Fizzy to help him finance and build a telephone line from Council to Nome. Thanks to Fizzy's perseverance and organizational skills, the line went through, offering a valuable service to the residents. But once again, Fizzy reaped no profits from her investment efforts.

The bright spot in her life was the arrival of her brother, Albert, from New York. Though not hardy enough for mining, he had an interest in newspaper work. Fizzy bought a half share in the *Council Daily News* so that Albert could learn the business.

Heavily in debt, Fizzy poured borrowed money into mining machinery and equipment, determined to make her claims pay. Many times she was tempted to give up and sell out. She nearly lost everything in August 1902 when she was given a week to pay her debt or lose her mine. "The week passed in a roar of water and a clatter of stones over the riffles of the sluice boxes and the clank of machinery," she wrote. "I was wet continually, but couldn't even take time to dry myself." In one week, Fizzy took out $40,000 in gold and paid off her claim. "During the following years, we cleaned up many times, but my thrill of that day in August . . . was never repeated."

Fizzy eventually took out over $100,000 dollars from her Ophir Creek claims, which she operated until 1906. While visiting Boston in 1906, she met John Sanger and married him seventeen days later. Sanger made one trip to Alaska, and announced he wouldn't stay there for all the gold in the world. So Fizzy sold her claims and left her little cabin in Council for good.

One wonders how she coped with the tameness of city life after she had endured so many adventures in the North, a place she came to love.

▼ *The cozy interior of Frances Fitz's cabin (1903) in Council City on the Seward Peninsula. Fabric and furs cover the bed and line the walls.*

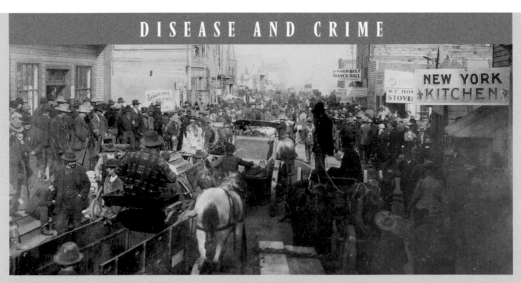

Nome, 1900.

Nome was built on swampy tundra that topped permanently frozen soil called permafrost. During the height of the gold rush, the city swelled to 15,000, most of whom were camped on the beach. What civil government existed was intermittent, and no sanitation measures were in place. Straw, paper, and discarded cloths, sheets, and blankets were thrown over the human waste that filled the alleys between and behind the saloons and gambling houses on Front Street. Nome was truly filthy.

Fears of an epidemic of typhoid or smallpox prompted the Chamber of Commerce to request that the Army declare martial law in June 1900. General Randall wrote, "Estimated this date, 16,000 people in the town and no effective civil organization for protection of life and property." He ordered a clean-up and appointed a health inspector. The general also ordered the construction of public latrines on high piers placed far enough out over the beach to allow the wastes to be carried out by high tide. Tickets for the latrines were sold at 10 cents each, or three for 25 cents.

In addition to the stench, filth, and threat of disease, gold rush Nome was a magnet for criminals, who had followed the gold seekers North. The Northwest Mounted Police warned the American authorities that many of the worst criminals ever known on this continent were en route to Nome in the fall of 1899. Among them were former members of Soapy Smith's gang in Skagway.

By August 1900 one observer wrote, "It is a conservative thing to say that Nome has within its limits the worst aggregation of criminals and unprincipled men and women that were ever drawn together in this country. The saloons and gambling houses, and the narrow streets and dark alleyways along the beach offer every opportunity to this class of criminals to successfully engage in their practices."

Frances Fitz, camped on the beach for the entire summer of 1900, wrote of the practice of chloroforming in which robbers subdued the sleeping occupants and made off with their gold.

Gold Rush Daughter

▲ *Klondy Nelson and her mother Alma, a Swedish immigrant, on their way to Nome in 1902. Klondy's father Warren, a perpetual prospector, named his baby daughter after the famous Klondike goldfields, just before he left for the Yukon in 1897.*

Two sailors held five-year-old Klondy Nelson high so the girl could catch her first glimpse of Nome as the barge crossed the harbor. From her father's letters she had pictured a fairy-tale city. But all she could see was a beach covered with gray tents and hundreds of men milling about, sorting through boxes and yelling out directions.

When Klondy and her mother Alma stepped off the barge, there was no one to meet them. No one resembled the man in the photograph she kept next to her bed in South Dakota. She had waited a long time to meet her father, Warren Nelson, who had left when she was a baby to search for gold in Alaska. Now she and her mother had journeyed to Nome to join him at his diggings, arriving on the last boat of the season in late October 1902.

The town of Nome, although three years old, seemed as impermanent as the sand the men were sifting—mostly a jumble of false-fronted buildings, half of which were saloons. Klondy and her mother stayed in Nome for several weeks, impatiently waiting for the ocean to freeze over so that they could make the trip across the sea ice by stagecoach and then overland by dogsled to the mining creeks at Ophir to rejoin the man they hadn't seen for five years.

Warren Nelson was not a successful miner. After his claim failed to pay out, he moved his family from the creeks at Ophir into the town of Council, where he briefly attempted to make a living as a storekeeper. But Klondy's father had wanderlust. And when he heard news of the discovery of the Third Beach at Nome in 1906, he staked the only paying claim he ever worked. The Solo Mine made enough that he could buy a pretty white house in Nome and move his family there.

Klondy enjoyed her Nome childhood. She studied the violin, learned to mush sled dogs, and befriended the Inupiat Eskimos who lived nearby. When Klondy was a teenager, her parents made plans for her to go to Denver to study violin. Around the same time her father predicted that all mining in the Nome area would soon be controlled by the big mining syndicates operating large gold dredges. The independent miners would be shut out, he said, just as they had been in Dawson.

So in the summer of 1911, Warren Nelson sold his claim and left Nome to prospect around Candle, on the other side of the Seward Peninsula. He assured his wife that he was leaving her with a big savings account. But when she went to the bank to withdraw the money for Klondy's trip to Colorado, she found there was no

▼ *As a teenager in Nome, Klondy fished for tom cod through the ice, a technique she learned from the her Inupiat neighbors.*

money. Klondy's father had cleaned out their accounts to outfit his latest mining quest. The people of Nome, determined not to let Klondy down, put on a benefit to raise money for her trip Outside.

Klondy's musical training was short-lived. She returned to Nome in the spring of 1912 to help her mother and brother, Ophir, run a boarding house from their home. They took in what lodgers they could, but the Nome rush was on the decline and fewer people needed accommodations.

In the autumn of 1913, high winds and pounding waves from a furious storm pummeled the Nome waterfront, destroying most of the buildings on Front Street. Two years later, when Klondy was eighteen, fewer than a thousand people remained in the once lively boomtown.

At the age of twenty Klondy moved to Seattle. Her mother refused to leave Alaska, believing that her husband would someday return. He did, once, on his way from Candle to a new strike on the Innoko. But it was too late. Alma Nelson had died a month before.

In 1922 Klondy married outdoorsman Frank Dufresne, a man she had known in Nome. Together they moved to Fairbanks, where Frank took a job as the first territorial wildlife agent. Klondy accompanied her husband and traveled throughout the territory by dog team and by riverboat, staying in the kind of one-room shanties Klondy thought she had left behind. Klondy and her family eventually settled in Juneau, where Frank became the first game commissioner of Alaska and they both wrote popular books about their adventuresome lives.

Some years later, Klondy met her father. "He still had the restless look of adventure in his face. 'I'm on my way to the Klondike,' he said. 'I hear they've just hit gold at Dawson. Nuggets as big as boulders. . . .' Never a word about Mother's lonely death, nothing about leaving us in Nome, nothing about my brother Ophir and me. He didn't mention my new husband. He didn't even ask if I had any children. His Viking blue eyes seemed to be fixed on something over the horizon, something no one else could see."

Two professional insurance brokers who arrived in Nome in 1900.

With the Klondike Gold Rush the biggest news in North America, major newspapers rushed their correspondents to Dawson to get firsthand reports. These journalists included Flora Shaw of the *Times* of London, Helen Dare of the *San Francisco Examiner,* and Alice Freeman writing as Faith Fenton for the *Toronto Globe.* And Emma Kelly wrote several stories about her gold rush adventures which were published in *Outdoor World* magazine.

The field of professional nursing was still new when the Victorian Order of Nurses sent some of their first members to the Klondike in 1898. Three members of the Sisters of St. Anne arrived shortly afterward. Thereafter nursing missionaries became the backbone of hospital staffs throughout the North.

Professional women were well established in the North by the time of the Nome gold rush in 1900. Businesswomen in Nome included mine owners, stenographers, and the insurance saleswomen pictured above.

Chapter 5

GOLD IN THE INTERIOR

WOMEN PAVE THE WAY

Unlike Nome and Skagway, gold rush Fairbanks was a law-abiding town. Women, many of whom were experienced stampeders from Dawson and Nome, were an essential part of Fairbanks' development from the beginning.

As news of Italian prospector Felix Pedro's 1902 gold discovery in the hills of the Tanana River valley spread, Fairbanks quickly grew from a makeshift trading post to a town of 500 houses with stores, hotels, saloons, sawmills, bathhouses, and a laundry. As in Dawson, women started hospitals, churches, and schools. Out on the gold creeks eight to twenty miles from Fairbanks were smaller towns: Dome City, Eldorado, Fox, Cleary, and Ester. By 1906, the Tanana Valley Railroad connected Fairbanks with the creek settlements.

The gold in the Fairbanks district was deep underground, but the prospectors on the creeks were all veterans of the many Northern gold rushes. They were prepared to stay and dig in, 15, 50, even 200 feet if necessary. Improvements in technology included steam boilers, which penetrated permafrost, thawing frozen soil by steam; and steam-driven winches that mechanically lifted paydirt from the shafts. But this kind of mining was expensive. It was no 'get rich quick' gold rush for the tenderfoot or cheechako.

Mining on a larger scale provided jobs for women, who cooked

◄◄◄ Fairbanks, on the Tanana River, while only two years old, was a bustling supply center for nearby mines in 1905.
◄◄ Like other Northern mining communities in the early 1900s, Fairbanks depended on the riverboats to deliver supplies and equipment from the Outside.
▲ Mrs. Kelly stands by the woodstove in her roadhouse on the Richardson Trail.

and waited tables at the larger mining camps and roadhouses, or operated hotels and businesses in Fairbanks and out on the creeks. Many women supported and cared for their families while their husbands were absent for months at a time, prospecting.

Gold production from the Fairbanks mining district jumped from $40,000 in 1903 to $600,000 in 1904, and to $6,000,000 in 1905. The settlement grew, reaching a population of over 3,000 by 1910. For many men and women who had drifted from camp to camp in the North for nearly a decade, Fairbanks became the place to settle permanently.

Although gold output decreased after 1909, Fairbanks continued to prosper as the center of trade in the region. More discoveries in the Interior of Alaska at Iditarod, in the remote Upper Koyukuk River region, and at Kantishna near Mount McKinley insured that the mining era continued in Alaska. These remote areas attracted

▼ *This early photo of Fannie Quigley was labeled "Mother McKenzie's Roadhouse" when it was taken in 1912 by Merl La Voy, of the Parker–Browne McKinley climbing expedition.*

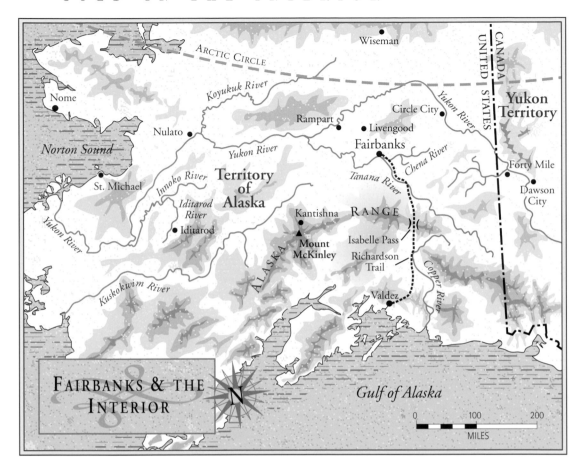

FAIRBANKS & THE
INTERIOR

frontier women like Nellie Cashman and Fannie Quigley, individualists who chose to make their way as miners, far from the comforts of civilization.

Alaska's last major strike occurred in Livengood in 1915, nearly twenty years after the first discoveries in the Klondike. A thousand or more eternally optimistic gold seekers traveled up tortuous streams in leaky boats, then tramped thorough miles of swamp to reach Livengood. Although hydraulic equipment and large-scale floating gold dredges were already in use in the Fairbanks and Circle Districts, the miners in Livengood built cabins and sank mine shafts, using techniques that had not changed much in twenty years.

ISABELLE CLEARY BARNETTE 1862–1942

First Lady of Fairbanks

▼ *Isabelle Barnette drives the golden spike for the Tanana Valley Railroad in July 1905, surrounded by men including Judge James Wickersham to her immediate left.*

In late summer 1901, Isabelle Barnette and her husband E. T., steamed up the Tanana River in a boat loaded with $20,000 in trade goods purchased in San Francisco. They were headed for Tanana Crossing, the site of the trading post they planned to build and the place they'd been told there would soon be a railroad station. Unfortunately, the small steamer could not navigate past treacherous Bates Rapids. Isabelle watched the gravelly river bars and forested banks slide by while E. T. and the Captain Adams, looking for a way around the rapids, argued unceasingly as the boat turned into Chena Slough.

As fate would have it, Captain Adams was unable to proceed farther upriver. Thus in late August 1901 the Barnette party and all their trade goods were cast out on the banks of the Chena six miles

ISABELLE C. BARNETTE

1862–1942

above at its confluence with the Tanana River. Wasting no time, the Barnettes and their crew built a trading post and prepared for the winter. While the new camp was hundreds of miles over rugged terrain from the nearest towns of Rampart and Circle City, there were already a few prospectors in the area.

That fall and winter, the Barnettes traded for furs with the local Athabascans. In March 1902, they left the trading post and set off for the Outside to purchase more supplies, each driving a dog team over the Alaska Range to the shipping port at Valdez. The little-used route crossed treacherous mountain passes pummeled by high winds and snow. Despite the difficult journey, a month later the unruffled Barnettes arrived in Valdez looking, according to one report, "like they had been on a Sunday drive."

Once in Seattle, the Barnettes restocked supplies and purchased a new steamboat. While they were gone, a prospector named Felix Pedro struck the mother lode on Pedro Creek, about sixteen miles north of the Barnette's trading post. By the time they returned in September, the Barnettes discovered, to their delight, that a small stampede had already started. E. T. quickly took advantage of the situation, promoting the location of the latest strike and his outpost, which he later named Fairbanks, in honor of an Indiana senator.

As the news spread, miners began to pour into Alaska's Interior from Dawson and Rampart. A few months later the camp was facing a food shortage, though many stampeders suspected that Barnette manufactured the shortage, hoarding supplies in his well-fortified cache so that he could sell his goods at a higher price. Angry miners threatened to hang one of Barnette's crew if he didn't sell his flour at a fair price. Isabelle found herself in the middle of an armed encampment when Barnette posted a guard of twelve men with rifles. While the frightening encounter ended in peaceful compromise, possibly due to Isabelle's presence in the compound, the miners always suspected Barnette of double-dealing.

With big strikes on Fairbanks and Cleary Creeks, in 1904 there was no doubt that Fairbanks was indeed the newest "Klondike in Alaska." A rough encampment of log cabins, tents, and saloons,

The pass through the Alaska Range, now the route for the Richardson Highway and the Alyeska Oil Pipeline, was named Isabelle Pass in commemoration of Isabelle Barnette's courageous 1902 dogsled journey.

Fairbanks attracted inhabitants who were veteran miners as well as their families. The town opened its first school in 1904, the same year that forty-two-year-old Isabelle bore her first child.

The Barnettes' claims and E. T.'s shrewd business dealings made the couple rich. As the wife of one of the wealthiest men in Fairbanks, Isabelle traveled widely. She and her sister accompanied Barnette to Washington, D.C., New York City, to Kentucky (where Barnette purchased a horse farm), and to Mexico (where he acquired a large plantation).

But trouble began brewing in Fairbanks. During the course of a lawsuit in 1906, it was revealed that E. T. had been convicted of a felony in Oregon in an 1886 horse trading deal gone bad. Whether this news was a revelation to Isabelle is unknown.

In 1910 Isabelle, now mother of two, moved to Los Angeles. The next year Barnette consolidated his Fairbanks Banking Company and the Washington Alaska Bank, then resigned from the enterprise and went to California. Just three months after he left, the bank collapsed and thousands of Fairbanks citizens lost their life savings. Barnette was indicted for embezzlement and was later tried in Valdez, but was found not guilty of all but one minor charge. Nevertheless, the people of Fairbanks never forgave Barnette for the bank's failure.

Isabelle had been a stalwart supporter of her husband through many lawsuits and downturns. But in 1918 Isabelle sued for divorce. The property settlement gave her a net worth of $500,000, a huge sum at the time.

Described as "the little woman," who was "frail and sometimes sickly," Isabelle Barnette put in more miles behind a dog team than most early pioneers, and was instrumental in the founding of Alaska's second-largest city. Judge James Wickersham, pioneer judge, politician, and adventurer who brought justice to Alaska's outposts, said of her, "Isabelle Barnette represents the highest type of that noble class of frontierswoman who have dared to risk their lives to assist in establishing the foundation for American states."

Mrs. Sullivan's roadhouse on the Richardson Trail, c. 1915.

The gold rush boomtowns of the Interior were accessible in the summer by riverboat, but winter travel was on foot or by dog team or horseback over frozen ground. An extensive trail system linking the Interior to other communities was served by stage companies. Travelers rode in open horse-drawn sleighs, wrapped in fur robes, their feet warmed by charcoal heaters. Every fifteen miles or so, or about a day's travel apart, was a roadhouse, which provided meals and beds for travelers, stables and feed for the horses, and bedding for the dog teams of mail and freight carriers.

As Fairbanks developed into the trading center of the Interior, the Richardson Trail became its lifeline to the Outside. Goods could be shipped year-round to Valdez, then freighted overland by dog teams 370 miles to the Interior.

For winter travelers, like Margaret Murie in 1918, the trip from Valdez to Fairbanks took seven to ten days, depending on the weather. Murie recalled Ma Sullivan's Roadhouse, about 278 miles from Valdez. Mrs. Sullivan tried to bring the refinements of civilized life to the wilderness by furnishing her home with "cretonne curtains at the windows, rag rugs on the floor, lots of fancy pillows on the big homemade sofa, floral lampshades on the oil lamps, and big old-fashioned rocking chairs with flowered cushions on them." Meals were a dollar or two; beds (a bunk if it was crowded, a cubicle if you were lucky) were $1.50 a night.

ERINIA PAVALOFF CHEROSKY CALLAHAN   1864–1955

Of Two Worlds

▲ *Erinia and Sergei Cherosky with their daughters Axinia and Helen at Circle City in 1898. Erinia became a respected business-woman in the Fairbanks community.*

To most of the citizens of Fairbanks in the 1940s, Grandma Callahan was just another old Native woman. Few stopped to wonder where she had come from, or knew how long she had lived in Fairbanks operating her well-respected skin-sewing business, or that she spoke Russian as well as several Native languages. And in a town that revered the gold rush and its pioneers, few realized how much Erinia Pavaloff Cherosky Callahan's life was intertwined with the gold strikes in the North.

She had worked for the famous traders, Harper, Mayo, and McQuesten, and had lived in all of the early camps: Fort Nelson, Fort Reliance, Belle Isle, Forty Mile. Her husband and brothers were responsible for the rich discoveries on Birch Creek and Little Minook, which started the gold rushes to Circle City and Rampart in 1894 and 1896.

She was born of two worlds, the daughter of an Athabascan woman and a half-Russian, half-Tlingit trader, who managed the Alaska Commercial Company trading post at Nulato. Her family combined subsistence methods for harvesting food with store-bought goods they purchased with the money they earned at the trading post.

At sixteen, Erinia married Sergei Cherosky, also of Russian and Athabascan descent. The young couple worked as translators for the traders, traveling with them as they explored the Yukon River Basin. Erinia befriended the traders' wives,

GOLD RUSH WOMEN

Kate McQuesten, Jennie Harper, and Margaret Mayo, and their children played together.

Grubstaked by Jack McQuesten, Erinia's husband, and her brother, Pitka Pavaloff, went upriver to prospect and to hunt moose in the summer of 1893. While prospecting in Birch Creek, they made a fantastic discovery. Erinia and her daughters joined the men at winter camp on Birch Creek. Over 100 white prospectors quickly followed them and, by the following spring, gold was discovered on many nearby creeks, including the fabulously rich Mammoth and Mastodon Creeks, named after the prehistoric dinosaur bones found there. Circle City quickly became the largest gold mining town on the Yukon River. Erinia moved to town and began a skin-sewing business while her daughters, Axinia and Helen, attended school with the children of traders and miners.

Unfortunately for Erinia and her husband, miners jumped their original claims, claiming that Pitka and Cherosky were not citizens because they were Native. Though Jack McQuesten interceded on their behalf, the Athabascan men lost their claims and were unwelcome in Circle City, the very settlement their discovery had created. Erinia had her skin-sewing business and adapted to the new situation, but she and Cherosky eventually parted.

In 1902 Erinia married freighter and miner Dan Callahan. They moved to Fairbanks in 1903, where Erinia continued her sewing business. She and her daughter Helen were among the first Native women to reside in the new town. Axinia and husband Nels Rasmussen ran a freighting business in Circle. Though Dan Callahan was elected to the Fairbanks city council and later the territorial legislature, Erinia and Helen were not always accepted in the white society of Fairbanks. As Alaska's gold rush society matured, social conventions became more rigid. Erinia and Callahan eventually separated, in part because Callahan failed to acknowledge his Native wife publicly.

Long active in the community, Erinia demonstrated that a Native woman could operate her own business in town. Helen lived with her mother until Erinia's death at the age of ninety-one.

NELLIE CASHMAN

A Mine of Her Own

▲ *Seventy-five-year-old Nellie Cashman, on a 1924 trip to Arizona just a year before her death.*

Irish-born Nellie Cashman was sixty years old in 1905 when she headed out from Fairbanks for the Koyukuk, the most remote gold placer district in North America. To reach her destination, she traveled by riverboat down the Tanana and the Yukon Rivers to Nulato, where she boarded a small flat-bottomed scow for the 500-mile journey up the Koyukuk River, then walked 50 miles overland to the site. Nellie reached Coldfoot on the Middle Fork of the Koyukuk River by midsummer. She was, as usual, staking claims, buying property, and leasing ground to work.

Nellie bought, sold, and traded mining properties like playing cards at an all-night poker game, a game which for her lasted half a century. A woman who preferred to live on frontiers, she had followed the gold rushes and boomtowns from Nevada and Arizona to California and the Arctic. Toward the end of her life, she was well-known for her spirited exploits and charitable deeds, the stories of which made good newspaper copy.

Her first trip North was in 1874. She joined the gold stampede in the Cassiar, a distinctive female form clad in a Mackinaw, men's trousers, and a fur hat. In the Cassiar, a mountainous region of northern British Columbia, she ran a boarding house and prospected for gold before returning to Victoria, British Columbia, for the winter. But hearing of starvation and scurvy among the prospectors left behind that winter, Nellie organized and led an expedition back into the mountains, a treacherous journey at that time of year. The supplies of potatoes and fresh vegetables she brought saved many from death, and wherever she went in later years, there was sure to be a miner who remembered her courage and compassion. She became known as the "Angel of the Cassiar."

From British Columbia, Canada, she went to

Tucson, Arizona, and ran the Delmonico Restaurant, the first white woman to open a business there. In 1880 she moved on to the newest of the mining camps—Tombstone, Arizona—and opened another restaurant. In addition to mining and running her businesses, Nellie constantly worked to solicit money for the church and for charity. She also became a mother to her five orphaned nieces and nephews.

Over the years, Nellie prospected and worked placer mines in New Mexico, Arizona, Montana, and Wyoming. "She worked like a Trojan in her search for riches," said her nephew, "and she was rewarded with modest wealth. But she was constantly giving it away to the poor and needy and various projects of her church."

Nellie heard news of the Klondike strike in September 1897. By March of the next year she was in Victoria, British Columbia, putting together an outfit, twenty-four years after her first trip North. A few weeks later she was headed over the Chilkoot Pass alone, hauling all her supplies herself, dressed practically as usual in men's clothing. Some reported that her fast talking got her past the Mounties without the required ton of goods.

Unlike the thousands wandering the streets of Dawson City, Nellie knew her way around a boomtown. She immediately opened another Delmonico Restaurant while on the lookout for claims to stake, lease, or buy. Her interest in the claim called No. 19 Below on Bonanza Creek eventually yielded a reported $100,000. (But she was also involved in various lawsuits related to other claims, and was even accused of trying to pass a bribe through Belinda Mulrooney!) Though she seemed to make a lot of money, she also spent a lot of money, giving it away to charitable causes and down-and-out miners.

In 1904, with Dawson in decline, Nellie followed the newest stampede to Fairbanks, where she opened a grocery store. Never far from a favorite charity, Nellie used a novel approach to gather donations for St. Matthew's Hospital in the new town. Comfortable around men in the mining camp saloons, Nellie would stake out a promising poker game. When the jackpot piled up sufficiently, she

Nellie Cashman poses with the younger "Alaska Nellie," Nell Lawing, in Seward, c. 1924. Lawing was the proprietor of a big game hunting lodge near Seward.

would reach into the middle of the table and sweep the money into her poke, saying, "Okay, boys! This is for the hospital. If you got the money to throw away at poker, you can give it to them hard-workin' Christian women that's takin' care of the sick." Meeting no resistance from stunned gamblers, she would move on to the next saloon and repeat her performance.

By 1907 Nellie was in Koyukuk country, having accumulated a block of claims on Nolan Creek, claims she developed and worked for the rest of her life. Every few years Nellie would travel Outside to sign up new investors, visit her nieces and nephews, and buy supplies. She often mushed the 350 miles to Nenana from her Wiseman claims by dog team.

When she arrived in Nenana in December 1923, after a seventeen-day mushing trip, newspapers all over the Alaska carried the story of the seventy-eight-year-old intrepid miner. Her nephew and his family in Bisbee, Arizona, urged her to retire and leave Alaska. She refused, declaring, "Those prospectors up there need me—and need me badly."

Back in Fairbanks again, Nellie hitched a ride on one of the first airplanes to make the trip back home. But the trips and the prospecting life were getting to be too much, even for Nellie. She contracted pneumonia.

Knowing it was the end, she asked to spend her last days at the hospital of her friends, the Sisters of St. Anne in Victoria, Canada. When she died in January 1925, she was eulogized in newspapers as far away as New York and Los Angeles as a grand old dame who staked a lasting claim on the hearts of miners throughout the West.

Gardening in Valdez in 1906.

Of the thousands of women who came North for gold rush riches in the 1890s, many retained a desire to make a home no matter where they found themselves. In the picture above, a Valdez woman creates a tight garden, a small plot of domesticity cultivated in a raw land. At that time, Valdez was a town of about 5,000, a seaport link at the beginning of the Richardson Trail to the Interior gold fields.

Author Annette Kolodny wrote in her book, *The Land Before Her,* that on the frontier, men saw wide open spaces, whereas "[women] dreamed more modestly of locating a home and a familial human community within a cultivated garden." In the North country of the gold rush era, this urge took many forms.

Scottish immigrant Peggy Shand sold her dowry and a farm near San Francisco to travel to the Klondike in 1897. She and her husband Davey never found riches, but for over thirty-two years she provided a home at their Stewart and Yukon River roadhouses for weary travelers passing through the Northland.

Swedish immigrant Alice McDonald tried to establish a home for herself and her children, first in Dawson and then in Fairbanks, while her husband Dan prospected for gold. Dan never hit it big, but Alice did when she left for the strike in Iditarod in 1910. First she started a hotel in a tent, then borrowed money to build the McDonald Hotel. In Iditarod, Alice became a mainstay of the community, known as Dr. McDonald for her knowledge of medicine.

FANNIE QUIGLEY

A Wilderness Life

▲ *Bohemian immigrant Fannie Quigley was well known for her wilderness life-style and her tasty cooking by the time this portrait was taken in Kantishna, c. 1935.*

Twenty-eight-year-old Fannie Sedlacek from Nebraska climbed over the Chilkoot Pass with the stampeders in 1898 and never left the North. Always one of the first on the scene of a new gold strikes, large and small, Fannie hiked into remote areas, pulling a sled laden with a tent, Yukon stove, and supplies, and hung out a shingle that stated, simply, MEALS. Far from Dawson and the refinements of civilization, her home-cooked meals earned her top dollar and the nickname, "Fannie the Hike." She prospected, too, even going as far as Clear Creek, over 100 miles from Dawson in the summer of 1900.

In October of that year, at age thirty she married Angus McKenzie. For a time they operated a roadhouse at No. 3 Below on Hunker Creek, just upstream from the small settlement of Gold Bottom. Problems with alcohol and violent arguments doomed the short-lived marriage. In January 1903 Fannie left Angus for good and set off on an 800-mile trek down the Yukon to Rampart, Alaska. Though she participated in many stampedes, she had little to show for it.

In August 1906 Fannie struck out for the new diggings in the Kantishna District, 175 miles from Fairbanks in the shadow of Mount McKinley, where she lived for the rest of her life. She staked numerous claims on Glacier Creek, where she met Joe Quigley, one of the miners who discovered the Kantishna mines. It was in Joe's cabin on his claim on upper Glacier Creek that Charles Sheldon, a big-game hunter from the East Coast, met Fannie in 1907. He and Harry Karstens found Joe's cabin empty, but went inside to wait, as was the Alaskan custom. Soon they heard someone coming, whistling, and to their surprise, a short bouncy woman banged open the door, and with much swearing, greeted them.

In addition to mining her claims, Fannie opened a roadhouse, really just a cabin where miners could pay for a good meal. Providing food for the table meant hunting, trapping, and growing as much as she could in her garden. Though she had never shot an animal until she lived in Kantishna, her prowess as a hunter became legendary. She hunted caribou, moose, sheep, and bears, butchered the meat expertly, and carried the meat on her back through the high hills to her home.

Her garden became famous throughout the area. Fannie's pansies, renowned for their size, occupied a prominent position in her garden, along with beets, cauliflower, cabbage, lettuce, onions, potatoes, radishes, rutabagas, rhubarb, and turnips. Poppies and many native wildflowers bloomed in profusion, according to geologist Stephen Capps, who visited in 1913.

Belmore Browne, who stopped by the cabin after his attempt to climb Mount McKinley in 1912, was served a memorable wilderness feast. "First came spiced, corned moose meat, followed by moose muffle jelly. Several varieties of jelly made from native berries covered the large slices of yeast bread, but what interested me more was rhubarb sauce made from the wild rhubarb of that region. . . . These delicacies were washed down with great bowls of potato beer, ice-cold from the underground cellar."

Joe and Fannie lived on their Glacier Creek claims until 1917. They were officially married by the commissioner in Eureka in 1918 and moved to the western end of Quigley Ridge, overlooking the confluence of Friday and Moose Creeks. Joe developed hard-rock claims, while Fannie had her own placer claims in Friday Creek.

By the early 1920s their claims were producing ore, and Fannie and Joe could afford to take a trip Outside, Fannie's first in all her years in the North. They visited Joe's family in Pennsylvania and some of Fannie's relatives in Nebraska.

▼ *Fannie Quigley grew her own produce, like this rhubarb, in the remote Kantishna mining country from 1907 until her death in 1944.*

The area adjoining their claims became part of Mount McKinley National Park in 1917. Fannie's old friend, Harry Karstens, was appointed as superintendent in 1921. Fannie's knowledge of the area proved invaluable to the young rangers, who often stopped at the Quigley cabin.

In 1930 Joe suffered a serious mining accident. During his rehabilitation, he met a young nurse. Things never were the same in their marriage, and Fannie never forgave him. In 1937, the claims were leased to the Red Top Mining Company, providing an income for Joe and Fannie, which they split as part of the divorce settlement. Joe married and moved to Seattle; Fannie remained in the country she loved, among the high hills.

Once accessible only by foot or by dog team, the McKinley National Park road was completed in the 1930s, opening Kantishna to visitors, park personnel, Alaska Road Commission staff, and the many dignitaries who came to call on Fannie. The small cabin overlooking Friday Creek, with her fenced garden and the dogs staked nearby, is pictured in many photographs from the era.

Toward the end of her life, Fannie became became a kind of curiosity around Mount McKinley. She lived alone, wore rough men's clothing, swore frequently, and habitually drank. Unable and unwilling to adapt to civilization, she preferred life away from cities. She was still waiting at her cabin to greet Bradford Washburn of Boston when he descended from his successful summit climb in 1942, as she had waited for climbers thirty years before.

Fannie died alone in her cabin in the summer of 1944.

► *Fannie still wore a traditional long black dress even while using her dogs to haul firewood in the early days at Glacier Creek, c. 1910.*

Epigraph

Klondy Nelson quote, p. 36.

Introduction

Klondike guides used include John Leonard's *Gold Fields of the Klondike,* 1897, and *Klondike: Chicago Record Book for Gold Seekers* (Monroe Book Company, 1897). Melanie Mayer's *Klondike Women* (Columbus: Swallow Press, Ohio University Press, 1989) was an important source.

1: Gold in the Yukon Basin

Introduction: Francois Mercier's *Recollections of the Youkon* [sic], edited by Linda Finn Yarborough (Alaska Historical Society, Anchorage, 1986), lists nearly 50 early traders before or contemporaneous with Harper, Mayo, and McQuesten. Also see Frances Backhouse's *Women of the Klondike,* (Vancouver/Toronto: Whitecap Books, 1995). *Sourdough Sagas* (Herbert Heller, ed., Comstock, Sausalito, 1967) includes important first-person accounts of prospecting

before 1885, especially the recollections of Henry Davis. The quote from Anna Fulcomer is from "The Three R's at Circle City," *Century* 66:2 (1898), p. 229.

On Native Women: Unfortunately, there is no history on these women. A short piece by Erinia Cherosky Callahan exists in the *Alaska Journal ,* 1975 ("A Yukon Autobiography," *Alaska Journal* 5, Spring 1975), pp. 127–128. Herbert Heller's *Sourdough Sagas* has important first-person accounts of the period before the Klondike gold rush, including one by Chris Sonnickson, who married Erinia Cherosky's sister Kate. Information about the traders is covered in Melody Webb's *The Last Frontier: A History of the Yukon Basin of Canada and Alaska* (University of New Mexico Press, Albuquerque, 1985) and in Michael Gates's *Gold at Fortymile Creek: Early Days in the Yukon* (University of British

Columbia Press, Vancouver, 1994.) Phyllis Fast's "Threads of Gold" exhibit folio (University of Alaska Museum, Fairbanks, 1997) discusses the importance of women in Koyokon Athabascan society and the possible basis for these women marrying non-Native traders and prospectors.

Katherine James McQuesten: Ironically in his reminiscences now published in pamphlet form by the Yukon Pioneers, Jack McQuesten never mentioned getting married *(Recollections of Leroy N. McQuesten: Life in the Yukon 1871–1885,* Yukon Order of Pioneers, Dawson City, 1952 and 1977). The Circle District Historical Society's vertical files, Mike Dalton, and descendants supplied information and confirmed dates.

Jennie Harper Alexander: Yvonne Mozee's biographical sketch on Walter Harper was published in the Seattle Mountaineers' edition of

Hudson Stuck's *Ascent of Denali.* Phyllis Fast, the Blair family, and other Harper descendants have been of assistance.

Anna De Graf: Information on Anna De Graf comes from her memoir *Pioneering on the Yukon,* edited by her great grandson, Roger Brown (Shoestring Press/Archon Books, Hamden, Connecticut, 1992); The quote (p. 27) is found on p. 12.

Bridget Mannion: Her life remains largely a mystery. The story "Bridget Struck it Rich" is from John Leonard's 1897 guidebook, *Gold Fields of the Klondike,* p. 140, but it offers no last name. Bridget's marriage to Frank Aylward is documented by Mike Gates in *Gold at Fortymile Creek.* We wishfully speculate that the story of "the unnamed servant girl who sued John J. Healy for her freedoms at the miner's meeting in Forty Mile," documented by Ogalvie, Gates (p. 89), and others is Bridget's story, but we cannot confirm this. To our knowledge, this "girl" remains unnamed in stories.

Emilie Tremblay: Her story was documented by Victoria Faulkner, courtesy of the Yukon Archives, and by Mike Gates, p. 86.

Crystal Snow: The Snow Family is documented in an extensive collection of papers at the Alaska State Library. A useful source was Rose Schneider's *The Snow Family of Juneau, Alaska: A Guide to the Papers and Photographs* (Alaska Department of Education, Juneau, 1992).

2: Klondike Discovery

Kate Carmack: Julie Cruikshank has explored the gold rush story from the perspective of the Native (First Nations) people in the Yukon in "Skookum Jim or Keish: Another View of the Klondike Gold Rush," a chapter in her book *Reading Voices: Oral and Written Interpretations of the Yukon's Past.* (Douglas and McIntyre, Vancouver, 1991). Mrs. Smith's quote is on page 133. Also Cruikshank's *Life Lived Like a Story* (University of Nebraska Press, Lincoln, 1990) was a helpful source. For George Carmack's story, see James A. Johnson's *Carmack of the Klondike* (Epicenter Press, Seattle, 1990).

Who found the gold? Barbara Kelcy reports in "Lost in the Rush: The Forgotten Women of the Klondike Stampede" (unpublished master's thesis, University of Victoria, 1989), p.143, the Armstrong story that Kate Carmack found the gold. The story that Kate accompanied George, Jim, and Charlie to Gold Bottom Creek, and on the return trip found the gold in Rabbit Creek is told in *The Alaska Yukon Gold Book: A Roster* (Sourdough Stampede Association, Seattle, 1930), p 30.

Ethel Berry: Her story is told in "How I Mined for Gold on the Klondyke" *(San Francisco Examiner Sunday Magazine,* August 1, 1897) and repeated in various Klondike guides. Alice Edna "Tot" Bush's *The Bushes and the Berrys* was privately published (C. J. Berry, San Francisco, 1941 and 1971) and covers the story of the two families only through the early gold rush years. Husband Clarence Berry's obituary was helpful, but we couldn't find an obituary for Ethel. Dates of birth and death are courtesy of the Berry family descendants, through William F. Berry.

Harriet Pullen: Information came from articles in the Alaska State Library's vertical file collection and Barrett Willoughby's *Alaskans All* (Houghton Mifflin, Boston, 1933). Further information was courtesy of Maxine Selmer.

Mollie Walsh Bartlett: Her story has been thoroughly researched and documented by Art Peterson and C. Scott Williams in *Murder, Madness, and Mystery: An Historical Narrative of Mollie Walsh Bartlett.* (Castle Peak Editions, Williams, Oregon, 1991). The Sourdough Jim Pitcher quote (p. 55) is from *Sourdough Jim Pitcher, The Autobiography of a Pioneer Alaskan* (Alaska Northwest Publishing Co., Anchorage, 1985), p. 21.

Lucille Hunter: Her story is documented only in her obituary in the *Whitehorse Star,* June 12, 1972. She was mentioned in Melanie Mayer's book Klondike Women. Lucille is also mentioned in *Gold and Galena* (Mayo Historical Society, 1990).

3: Dawson City

Belinda Mulrooney: Belinda Mulrooney was discussed in an article by Robert DeArmond in the *Fairbanks Daily News Miner* (March 11, 1990, section C, p.1). Primary sources include a variety of old newspaper articles from Dawson papers. This material is also covered by Mayer and Backhouse. A biography is being completed by DeArmond and Melanie Mayer.

Martha Louise Munger Black: Her memoir *My Ninety Years* (Alaska Northwest Publishing Co., Anchorage, 1976) is a beloved Klondike classic; the quote (p. 71) can be found on pp. 29-30.

Klondike Kate Rockwell: The story of Kate Rockwell, a vigorous self promoter, has been retold many times. The Yukon Archives has put together a useful bibliography. Ellis Lucia wrote a fictionalized biography titled *Klondike Kate* (Comstock, Sausalito, 1962). Also the series "Memories of Klondike Kate" by Rov Schillios was featured in the *Alaska Sportsman* and included the articles "Dance Hall Girl" (March 1956), p. 8 ff., and "Dreams and Reality" (April 1956), p.16 ff. For more about the lives of dancehall girls and prostitutes, see Frances Backhouse's *Women of the Klondike* , chapter 5.

4: Beyond the Klondike

Margaret Mayo: Details of her life have been supplied by great-granddaughter Barbara Nelson, a diligent collector and custodian of family history. Margaret is mentioned in Josie Earp's *I Married Wyatt Earp: The Recollections of Josephine Sarah Marcus Earp* , edited by Glenn G. Boyer (Tucson, University of Arizona Press, 1976), pp. 169–170.

Nome: For the story of the new town, see Terrence Cole's *Nome: City of the Golden Beaches* (Vol. 11, No. 1, Alaska Geographic Society, Anchorage, 1984).

Sinrock Mary: Information on Sinrock Mary was obtained from a video by Maria Brooks, KAKM TV, and from Pat Partnow's teaching guide

Natives in Alaska's History (Anchorage School District, Indian Education Program, June 1984), pp. 42–44. Also see Dorothy Jean Ray's article "The Making of a Legend: Charlie and Mary Antisarlook's Reindeer Herd," *Ethnohistory in the Arctic: The Bering Strait Eskimo),* pp. 118–119. Sinrock Point was 27 miles west of the present site of Nome. Sinrock is an anglicized word taken from the Eskimo word singuk (or chinik in Yup'ik) meaning "point." Though she only lived there seven years of her life, the name Sinrock Mary followed her.

Josephine Marcus Earp: Josie told her story to two of Wyatt's nieces. From these manuscripts Glenn Boyer created *I Married Wyatt Earp: The Recollections of Josephine Sarah Marcus Earp* (Glenn G. Boyer, ed., University of Arizona Press, Tucson, 1976); the quotes (p. 88) are from pp. 163-64. Boyer's notes in that volume are invaluable. See also *Wyatt Earp: Facts Volume Two* by Glenn G. Boyer (Historical Research Associates, Rodeo, New Mexico, 1996). For more about the Jewish experience in the West, see *Pioneer Jews: A New Life in the Far West* by

Harriet and Fred Rochlin (Houghton Mifflin, Boston, 1984).

Frances Ella Fitz: She recounted her story in the book *Lady Sourdough,* as told to Jerome Odlum (Macmillan, New York, 1941); the quote (p. 94) is from p. 316. Quotes (p. 95) are from Terrence Cole's *Nome: City of Golden Beaches* (pp. 73-74).

Klondy Nelson Dufresne: She told her story with the assistance of Corey Ford in the popular book *Daughter of the Gold Rush* (Random House, New York, 1955); the quote (p. 98) is from p. 169.

5: Gold in the Interior

Isabelle Cleary Barnette: For a history of Fairbanks and information about Isabelle, see Terrence Cole's *Crooked Past: The Strange Story of E. T. Barnette* (Fairbanks, University of Alaska Press, 1992). Also, see *Old Yukon: Tales Trails and Trials* by Judge James Wickersham (Washington Law Book Co., Washington, D.C., 1938); *Fairbanks Weekly News,* April 16, 1904; May 7, 1904; "Arrival of Baby Girl", noted July 30, 1904; and the speech by Wickersham, July 18, 1905. Information also contained in "The Lady was a Trailblazer " by Robert DeArmond, *Alaska Sportsman,* July

1958, pp. 30–31. The quote on page 109 is from Margaret Murie's *Two in the Far North* (Seattle, Alaska Northwest Books, 1978), p. 65.

Erinia Pavaloff Cherosky Callahan: The Circle District Historical Society files collected by the late Pat Oakes were invaluable; they include articles by Lone E. Janson and many others about Minook, Pitka, Erinia, and her daughters. Pat Partnow's article on Erinia in *Natives in Alaska's History* (Anchorage School District, Indian Education Program, June 1984), pp. 39–41 was helpful. The obituary of Helen Callahan is featured in the July 10, 1977, edition of the *Fairbanks Daily News Miner.* Erinia tells her own story in "A Yukon Autobiography," *Alaska Journal* (Spring 1975), pp. 127–128. Mary Warren has collected and shared valuable information. Bob King provided dates and information through personal communication and his unpublished research.

Sidebar, page 115. The quote is from Annette Kolodny's *The Land Before Her* (Chapel Hill, University of North Carolina Press, 1984).

Nellie Cashman: See Don Chaput's book *Nellie*

Cashman and the North American Mining Frontier (Westernlore Press, Tucson, 1995) for information and an extensive bibliography. The story of Nellie's unique fundraising efforts is from Clara Heintz Burke's book *Doctor Hap* (Coward McCann, New York: 1961), p. 91. John Cook of the Bureau of Land Management and George Lounsbury of Fairbanks provided information about Nellie's life in Alaska. For more about women miners and prospectors see *A Mine of Her Own* by Sally Zanjani (Swallow Press, 1997).

Fannie Quigley: Fannie Quigley is the subject of a biography by Jane Haigh, unpublished manuscript. Her obituary was published in the *Fairbanks Daily News Miner,* August 1944. Story about Sheldon and Karstens is from Margaret Murie, personal communication. See Belmore Browne's article in *Outing Magazine,* July 1913, p. 399; Mary Lee Davis's book *We Are Alaskans* (Wilde and Co., Boston, 1931), p. 199; and Grant H. Pearson's book with Philip Newill, *My Life of High Adventure* (Prentice Hall, Englewood Cliffs, N. J., 1962).

FURTHER READING

Backhouse, Frances. *Women of the Klondike.* Vancouver/Toronto: Whitecap Books, 1995.

Berton, Laura. *I Married the Klondike.* Toronto: McClelland and Stewart, 1961.

Berton, Pierre. *Klondike Fever.* New York: Alfred A. Knopf, 1958.

Black, Martha Louise. *My Ninety Years.* Anchorage, Alaska Northwest Publishing Company, 1976.

Chaput, Don. *Nellie Cashman and the North American Mining Frontier.* Tucson: Westernlore Press, 1995.

Cole, Terrence. *Crooked Past: The Strange Story of E. T. Barnette.* Fairbanks: University of Alaska Press, 1992.

Cole, Terrence. Nome: *"City of the Golden Beaches."* Anchorage: Alaska Geographic Society, Vol. 11, No. 1, 1984.

Cruikshank, Julie. *Life Lived Like a Story.* Lincoln: University of Nebraska Press, 1990.

Cruikshank, Julie. *Reading Voices: Oral and Written Interpretations of the Yukon's Past.* Vancouver: Douglas and McIntyre, 1991.

De Graf, Anna. Edited by Roger S. Brown. *Pioneering on the Yukon.* Hamden, Conn.: Shoestring Press, 1992.

Earp, Josephine. Edited by Glenn G. Boyer. *I Married Wyatt Earp: The Recollections of Josephine Sarah Marcus Earp.* Tucson: University of Arizona Press, 1976.

Fitz, Frances Ella, as told to Jerome Odlum. *Lady Sourdough.* New York: Macmillan, 1941.

Gates, Michael. *Gold at Fortymile Creek: Early Days in the Yukon.* Vancouver: University of British Columbia Press, 1994.

Heller, Herbert, ed. *Sourdough Sagas.* Sausalito: Comstock, 1967.

Johnson, James A. *Carmack of the Klondike.* Seattle: Epicenter Press, 1990.

Luchetti, Cathy, and Carol Olwell. *Women of the West.* New York: Orion Books/Library of the American West, 1982.

Lucia, E. *Klondike Kate.* Sausalito: Comstock, 1962.

Mayer, Melanie. *Klondike Women: True Tales of the 1897–1898 Gold Rush.* Columbus: Swallow Press/Ohio University Press, 1989.

Peterson, Art, and C. Scott Williams. *Murder, Madness, and Mystery: An Historical Narrative of Mollie Walsh Bartlett.* Williams, Ore.: Castle Peak Editions, 1991.

Rochlin, Harriet, and Fred Rochlin. *Pioneer Jews: A New Life in the Far West.* Boston: Houghton Mifflin, 1984.

Shand, Margaret Clark, and Ora M. Shand. *The Summit and Beyond.* Caldwell, Idaho: Caston Printers, 1959.

Webb, Melody. *The Last Frontier: A History of the Yukon Basin of Canada and Alaska.* Albuquerque: University of Mexico Press, 1985.

Willoughby, Barrett. *Alaskans All.* Boston: Houghton Mifflin, 1933.

Wold, JoAnne. *The Way It Was.* Seattle: Alaska Northwest Books, 1988.

Wold, JoAnne. *This Old House.* Seattle: Alaska Northwest Books, 1978.

Zanjani, Sally. *A Mine of Her Own.* Lincoln: University of Nebraska Press, 1997.

PHOTO CREDITS

ASL: Alaska State Library.
UAF: Archives, Alaska and
　　　Polar Regions
　　　Department, University
　　　of Alaska Fairbanks.
YA: Yukon Archives,
　　　Whitehorse.

Front cover: Right— Courtesy
of William F. Berry. Left (top to
bottom)—Courtesy of Candy
Waugaman, Roger Brown,
Candy Waugaman, and YA.
Page 3: From Klondy Nelson's
Daughter of the Gold Rush,
courtesy of Judy Grimes.
4: Courtesy of Roger Brown.
4: UAF, Stephen Foster
Collection #69-92-22.
5: UAF, Stephen Foster
Collection #69-92-595.
8: UAF, Vertical File #896-38N.
10: YA, H.C. Barley Collection.
11: Courtesy of Candy
Waugaman.
12: ASL.
13: Courtesy of Candy
Waugaman.
16: UAF, Vertical File Forty
Mile #76-132-15N.
18: UAF, VF #58-1026-766N.
19: YA, T. R. Lane photo.
20: Courtesy of Candy
Waugaman.
24: Courtesy of Barbara Nelson.
26: Courtesy of Roger Brown.
28: UAF Rare Books,

photographer Veazie Wilson's
Glimpses of Alaska.
29: Fort Yukon: UAF, Vertical
File #58-1026-1729.
30: Courtesy of Kathleen
Donahue.
32: UAF Rare Books, Veazie
Wilson's *Glimpses of Alaska.*
33: UAF, Vertical File #61-
1022-42.
34: ASL, PCA 154.115.
35: UAF Rare Books, Veazie
Wilson's *Glimpses of Alaska.*
36: Chilkoot Pass: ASL, J. M.
Blackenberg Collection, PCA
125-22.
38: Courtesy of William F. Berry.
39: UAF, Dawson Photo
Collection #67-107-2.
43: UAF, J. B. Moore
Collection #76-35-26N.
44: YA.
45: YA.
46: Courtesy of Candy
Waugaman.
48: Courtesy of William F. Berry.
50: Courtesy of William F. Berry.
51: ASL, Winter and Pond
photo #87-661.
52: Courtesy of Candy
Waugaman.
53: Courtesy of Candy
Waugaman.
54: Courtesy of Candy
Waugaman.
56: UAF, McKay Collection
#70-58-268N.

58: YA, Harrington Collection
#105.
60: UAF, Charles Bunnell
Collection #58-1026-1634N.
62: ASL, Winter and Pond
photo, PCA 87-682.
63: UAF, McKay Collection
#70-58-269N.
64: UAF, Vertical File.
66: Courtesy of Candy
Waugaman.
68: UAF, Lindberg Collection.
69: UAF, Albert Johnson
Collection #89-166-05N.
70: YA, MLB Collection #3258.
73: YA, MLB Collection #3259.
74: Courtesy of Candy
Waugaman.
77: UAF, Barrett Willoughby
Collection.
78: UAF, Vertical File #64-92-
734.
80: ASL, B. B. Dobbs #122-30.
81: UAF, Vertical File,
Roadhouses #63-40-137N.
84: Courtesy of Barbara Nelson.
85: Courtesy of Barbara Nelson.
86: Courtesy of Candy
Waugaman.
87: UAF, Zug Album #80-68-
341N.
88: Arizona Historical Society.
89: UAF, Charles Bunnell
Album #58-1026-1692N.
91: ASL, Dobbs Collection
#12-72.
92: *Lady Sourdough* (New York:

The Macmillan Co., 1941).
94: *Lady Sourdough* (New York:
The Macmillan Co., 1941).
95: UAF, Seppala Album.
96-97: Courtesy of Judy Grimes.
99: Courtesy of Terence Cole.
100: UAF, Charles Bunnell
Collection.
102: UAF, Charles Bunnell
Collection #58-1026-1531N.
103: UAF, James Geoghegan
Collection.
104: UAF, Farquhar Collection.
106: UAF, T. Cole Folder,
VFSC #76-38-2N.
109: UAF, James Geoghegan
Collection.
110: Courtesy of Josephine
Roberts.
112: Arizona Historical Society.
114: UAF, Lulu Fairbanks
Collection #68-69-526.
115. UAF, Mary Whalen
Collection #75-84-47.
116: UAF, Stephen R. Capps
Collection.
117: UAF, Fannie Quigley
Collection.
118: UAF, Fannie Quigley
Collection.
119: Courtesy of Terrence Cole.
122: Courtesy of Candy
Waugaman.
123: Courtesy of YA, H. C.
Barley Collection.
124: ASL.

INDEX

INDEX

ACKNOWLEDGMENTS

Living virtually next door to the Rasmuson Library has made this book possible. Their Alaskana collection has virtually every Klondike Guide and every first-person account available. All of the librarians, especially Ron Inouye, Gretchen Lake, Marge Naylor, and Phyllis Movius, have been extremely helpful. Also thanks to the research staff at the Noel Wien Library in Fairbanks, Candy Waugaman, Evelyn Friske, Donna Krier, Mike Gates, the staff of the Yukon Archives and the Dawson City Museum in Dawson, Judy Kleinfield, Melanie Mayer, Jane Williams and the Circle District Historical Society, Bob King, Phyllis Fast, William F. and Neva Berry, Barbara Nelson, Miranda Wright, Roger Brown, Kevin Mann, the staff of the Circle Museum, Elva Scott, John Cook, George Lounsbury, the late Pat Oakes, Pat Partnow, Kay Shelton and the research staff at the Alaska State Library, Effie Kokrine, Mary Warren, Terrence Cole, Wanda Chin, Terry Dickey, and the University of Alaska Museum staff.

CLAIRE RUDOLF MURPHY has written more than fifteen books for children, fiction and nonfiction, including *I am Sacajawea, I Am York: Our Journey West with Lewis and Clark; Children of Alcatraz* and her latest book *Marching with Aunt Susan: Susan B. Anthony and the Fight for Women's Suffrage*. Claire has a passion for history, especially the untold stories of outsiders. During her years in Alaska, she taught language arts and drama, and worked with the Alaska State Writing Project. Currently Claire serves on the faculty of Hamline University's MFAC, a graduate creative writing program for children's writers. She lives in Spokane, Washington, where she enjoys music and outdoor activities with her husband. Her two grown children live in Seattle.

www.clairerudolfmurphy.com
www.thestorytellersinkpot.blogspot.com

Claire Rudolf Murphy, left, and Jane G. Haigh.

Alaska author and historian **JANE HAIGH** began her career as a local historian in Fairbanks where she completed an MA in Northern Studies at the University of Alaska Fairbanks. She was honored in 2007 as the Alaska Historian of the Year by the Alaska Historical Society for her most recent books, *Searching for Fannie Quigley: A Wilderness Life in the Shadow of Mt. McKinley* (Ohio University Press, 2007) and *King Con: the Story of Soapy Smith* (Friday 501 Books, 2006). Jane recently completed a PhD in U.S. History and American Indian Studies at the University of Arizona in Tucson and has joined the faculty at Kenai Peninsula College, in Soldotna, Alaska.

www.janehaigh.com